Oregon
CURIOSITIES

Help Us Keep This Guide Up to Date

Every effort has been made by the author and editors to make this guide as accurate and useful as possible. However, many things can change after a guide is published—establishments close, phone numbers change, hiking trails are rerouted, facilities come under new management, etc.

We would love to hear from you concerning your experiences with this guide and how you feel it could be made better and be kept up to date. While we may not be able to respond to all comments and suggestions, we'll take them to heart and we'll also make certain to share them with the author. Please send your comments and suggestions to the following address:

Globe Pequot Press
Reader Response/Editorial Department
P.O. Box 480
Guilford, CT 06437

Or you may e-mail us at:
editorial@GlobePequot.com

Thanks for your input, and happy travels!

Curiosities Series

Oregon
CURIOSITIES

Quirky characters,
roadside oddities &
other offbeat stuff

2nd Edition

Harriet Baskas

Guilford, Connecticut

The prices, rates, and hours listed in this guidebook were confirmed at press time. We recommend, however, that you call establishments to obtain current information before traveling.

To buy books in quantity for corporate use
or incentives, call **(800) 962–0973**
or e-mail **premiums@GlobePequot.com.**

Photos by Harriet Baskas unless otherwise noted.

Maps by Daniel Lloyd © Morris Book Publishing, LLC

Text design: Bret Kerr

Layout: Casey Shain

Project editor: John Burbidge

Library of Congress Cataloging-in-Publication data is available on file.

ISBN 978-0-7627-4971-3

Printed in the United States of America

10 9 8 7 6 5 4 3 2 1

*For Ross, who first lured me to Oregon and made sure
I found my way back there.
In memory of my mom, who told me to be a person and
not a pair of pants, and my dad, who taught me to pay
attention. And for David and Elliot: Team Baskas.*

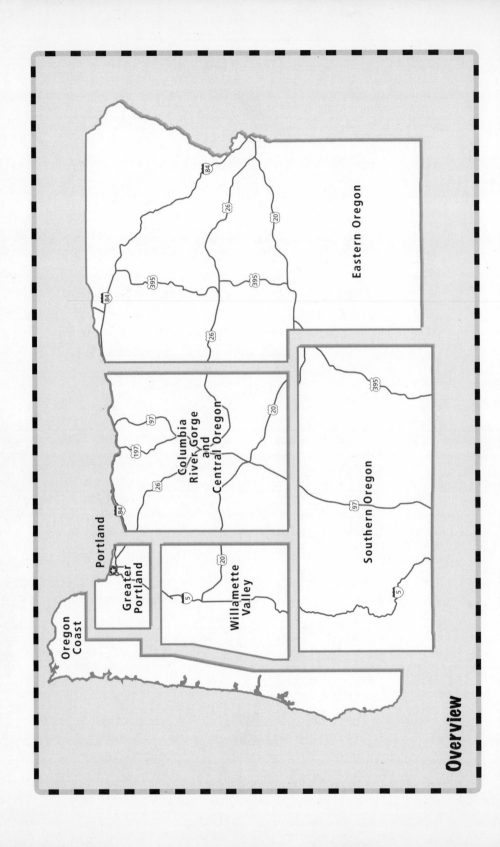

Overview

contents

acknowledgments

*T*hanks to Emma Schwartzman, Helen Lennon Moore, and Charlene Cuhaciyan for research and organizing help; Allen Jones for his excellent copyediting; David Schargel of Portland Walking Tours for his generosity; Heidi Lagao of www.kolshots.com and the many other folks who offered tips and shared photos; and to the staff and volunteers at the chambers of commerce and visitor centers who patiently answered all my curious questions. And giant thanks to friends near and far who shared (or pretended to share) my glee over encounters with the Goddess of Leisure, the World's Largest Oyster Cracker, the bowling ball tree, the giant ball of string, and everything else in this very curious book.

introduction

★ ★

*I*t started with a stump house and careened out of control with the giant hairball.

My attraction, appreciation, and devotion to finding unusual people, places, and things in Oregon started when I first arrived in 1980. On the drive across country I'd practiced saying OR-eh-gun instead of Or-e-GONE and had it down by the time we rolled into Portland. I thought it would be easy to blend in, but I wasn't prepared for what I'd find when I began exploring.

First stop: the Pacific Ocean. Actually, it took a long time for me to make it to the ocean because I got distracted on the way there by the Tillamook County Pioneer Museum, where thousands of odds and ends (mostly odds) are displayed in every nook and cranny of an old courthouse. After marveling at the Native American basketry collection, I was thoroughly charmed by the purple, green, and blue carnival-glass tumbler labeled "Elmer Snook's most prized possession." But I was hooked when I spotted Joseph Champion's stump.

Joe Champion's "castle" is long gone, but it has been recreated at the Tillamook County Pioneer Museum.
Tillamook County Pioneer Museum

introduction

★ ★

Visitors to the stump house add some perspective on its size.
Tillamook County Pioneer Museum

Champion, who in 1851 was possibly Tillamook's first white settler, needed a place to live. So he set up house in the stump of a huge, hollow spruce tree and declared it his "castle." The actual stump is long gone, but the museum has re-created it. And right beside the pseudo-stump is a very real photo that shows three women standing in the stump's "doorway" with their outstretched arms across the opening. That unusual "house," that hard-to-believe picture, and the realization that there were once stumps in the Oregon woods big enough to live in got me thinking about what other unusual things might be out there.

As it turns out, there are quite a few. Way more, in fact, than can ever fit into a book. I found natural geological wonders, including spots called simply Hole-in-the-Ground and Crack-in-the-Ground. I discovered hand-hewn wonders such as the magical Petersen Rock Garden in Redmond and the fanciful Fun Farm in Bend. I learned about wacky events, including the Jell-O Art Show in Eugene, the Rooster Crowing Contest in Rogue River, and the frog-jumping contest in Milton-Freewater. And then there were the "things." The building shaped like a jug. The World's Shortest River. The World's Smallest Park. And the World's Tallest Barber Pole. And what may very well be the World's Largest Hairball.

Ah, the hairball. It's my favorite thing in the world. Not just because it weighs in at two and a half pounds. (Well, that's pretty wonderful right there.) Not just because it was discovered in the belly of a hog at a meatpacking plant in the 1940s. (Gross, yes, but really sort of cool.) But because someone realized that this giant hairball was special and thought that the monks at the museum at the Mount Angel Abbey would be happy to see it. They were, and they placed the hairball alongside their taxidermied two-headed calf. And then they left it up to us to decipher the meaning.

Over the years I've made several pilgrimages to that hairball. Alone and with friends. And no, the hairball doesn't "speak" to me or anything like that. I'm just glad that, like the other Oregon curiosities in this book, this unusual object is being well looked after so we can all visit and make up our own minds about the meaning. Or just be entertained and amazed.

Overall, it's been a blast touring Oregon hunting for the unusual. The search for "tidbits" was especially entertaining and educational. I learned, for example, that the Oregon state flag is the only state flag with a different design on each side. (One side has a beaver, which reflects the state's nickname. The other has the date, 1859, that Oregon was admitted to the union.) And I was reminded that Oregon is still one of only two states where you may not pump your own gas. (The other holdout is New Jersey.) And I hadn't quite realized how "official" Oregon is: Milk is the official state beverage, the square dance is the official state dance, and the chinook salmon is the official state fish. It doesn't stop there. The Oregon grape is the official state flower, the Douglas fir is the official state tree, and the Oregon swallowtail is the official state insect. Oregon also has an official nut (the hazelnut), an official fossil (the metasequoia), and an official mushroom (the Pacific golden chanterelle).

I'm working on getting that hairball added to the list.

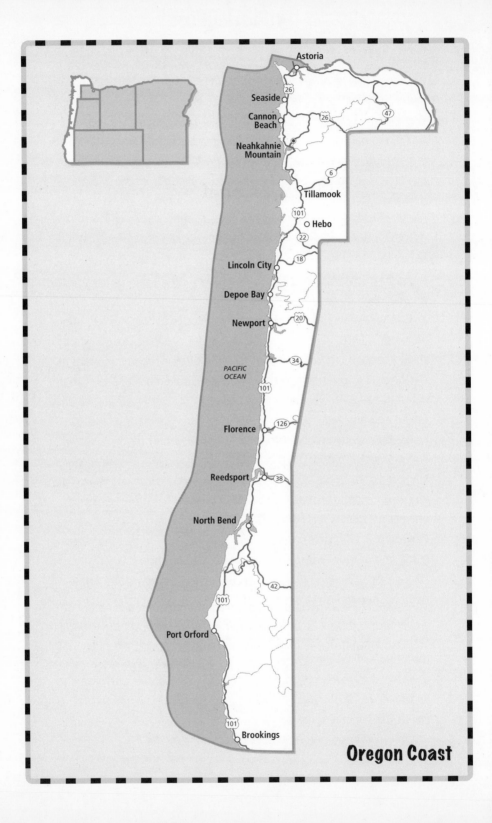

Astoria

26

47

Seaside

26

Cannon
Beach

6

Neahkahnie
Mountain

Tillamook

101

○ Hebo

22

18

Lincoln City

Depoe Bay

Newport

20

34

PACIFIC
OCEAN

101

Florence

126

Reedsport

38

North Bend

42

101

Port Orford

101

Brookings

Oregon Coast

CHAPTER

1

Oregon Coast

The Oregon coast stretches 400 miles along US 101, from Astoria at the ship-eating mouth of the Columbia River down to balmy Brookings, just north of the California border. Along the way you'll find lovely beaches, dense forests, rolling dunes, and plenty of tourist towns and distractions. As you poke around, keep an eye out for the World's Shortest River, a park devoted to carnivorous cobra lilies, and the spot where a washed-up, dead whale once exploded, smashing a car and covering onlookers with icky whale goop.

The coast is also where you can visit a park filled with huge, home-made dinosaurs painted in unusual colors and see some of the sites where scenes in The Goonies, Kindergarten Cop, and Free Willy were shot. If you're brave, you can spend time at haunted roadsides, restaurants, and fire stations. Armed with binoculars, you can gaze out at sea to the historic, decommissioned lighthouse that now serves as a columbarium.

And if you stop in Newport, at the Oregon Coast History Center, you can marvel over a foghorn fashioned from a tuba, an arched bridge made from toothpicks, and a portrait of Miss Electricity, the young lady who way back in 1891 was willing to be wired up with a garland of light bulbs, a light-bulb-topped crown, and a scepter studded with light bulbs to prove to the community that electricity was indeed safe.

★ ★

Bridge to Nowhere?

Astoria

Just beyond Astoria where the Columbia River rushes to meet the Pacific Ocean, there have been so many shipwrecks and drownings in the treacherous, stormy waters that the area has been dubbed the "Graveyard of the Pacific."

At its widest the mouth of the Columbia is 10 miles across, but from Astoria it's "just" a tad over 4 miles to the Washington side. And on a clear, calm day it's easy to imagine how thrilling it could be to make your way across the river the way folks did back in the mid-to-late 1800s: in the homemade passenger and cargo "ferry" a local schoolteacher built out of two canoes he strapped together.

But the river is rarely calm: The current can run at close to 10 miles per hour, and the winds can whip at more than 100 miles per hour.

The 4.1-mile "bridge to nowhere" is the longest continuous truss bridge in the world. Oregon Department of Transportation

★ ★

So it was a happy day when an actual boat replaced the canoe-ferry and no doubt cause for celebration when, in 1946, the state of Oregon began offering scheduled ferry service on the half hour, in good weather only.

Then someone had a better idea: Why not build a bridge? Not just any bridge, but the longest continuous truss bridge in the world and a structure that could withstand winds of up to 150 mph.

At first, politicians dismissed the idea as frivolous and truly unnecessary. But when the 4.1-mile Astoria-Megler Bridge opened on August 27, 1966, more than 30,000 people, including Miss Oregon and Miss Washington, showed up for the cutting of the ceremonial ribbon for the "bridge to nowhere." And nowhere turned out to be somewhere: 240,000 toll-paying vehicles crossed the bridge during the first five months it was open, and by 1993 enough tolls had been collected so that the bridge bonds were retired a full two years early.

On stormy and windy days it can still be a bit scary crossing the river on the bridge, but at least these days the crossing is not only thrilling—it's free.

History on a Stick

Astoria

In Rome, Emperor Trajan, his battles, and his conquests are honored with an elegant marble column built in 113 AD. Known today as Trajan's Column, the pillar is extensively illustrated with an elaborate spiral of relief carvings created using an etching technique known as sgraffito.

No need to travel to Italy to see what something like this looks like. In 1926 the folks in Astoria decided to commemorate the city's role in the conquest of the West with their own 125-foot-tall monument patterned after Trajan's Column.

Built on Coxcomb Hill, the highest spot in town, the Astoria Column was made of reinforced concrete, not marble. But at $30,000,

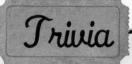
Arcane Astoria

- Astoria was the first—and is the oldest—permanent U.S. settlement west of the Rockies.

- Astoria sits at the mouth of the Columbia River. Called the "Graveyard of the Pacific," the Columbia River Bar has claimed approximately 2,000 vessels and 700 lives.

- Fort Clatsop was the winter encampment site of the Lewis and Clark Expedition and is the oldest U.S. military fort on the West Coast. In 2005 a replica of the original fort burned to the ground, but a new historically accurate structure was quickly rebuilt.

- Fort Stevens, 10 miles west of Astoria, is the only military installation in the continental United States to be fired on by a foreign power since the War of 1812. Shells were discharged from a Japanese submarine during World War II. There was no damage, and Fort Stevens did not return fire.

- Clark Gable performed at The Astoria Theater in the summer of 1922, long before he became a famous Hollywood film star. The theater no longer exists.

At low tide in nearby Hammond, the remains of the *Peter Iredale* are a tourist attraction.
Astoria-Warrenton Chamber of Commerce

★ ★

the price tag wasn't cheap. Luckily the bill was picked up by the Great Northern Railroad and the great-grandson of John Jacob Astor, the millionaire fur trader for whom the town is named.

Recently refurbished for quite a bit more than $30,000, the unusual column sports a lovely and (don't tell the kids) educational spiral mural etched with fourteen scenes from the area's early history, including the "discovery" of the Columbia River by sea captain Robert Gray in 1792, the arrival of fur traders and other white settlers, and (what a surprise) the establishment of the railroad in

History can spiral up or down.
Astoria-Warrenton Chamber of Commerce

the nineteenth century. And while the outside of the column is an impressive sight, on a clear day there's an extra reward for those who climb the 164-step interior spiral staircase to the viewing platform: spectacular views of timber-covered hillsides, the Astoria Bridge, the Columbia River, and, on truly clear days, the Pacific Ocean.

The Astoria Column is open daily from dawn until dusk. From downtown Astoria take Sixteenth Street to Jerome and turn right. Go 1 block and turn left on Fifteenth Street, then left again on Cox- comb Drive, which leads to the column. For more information call the Astoria-Warrenton area Chamber of Commerce at (800) 875-6807 or the Astoria Column gift shop at (503) 325-2963 or visit www.astoria column.org.

Filmed Here

According to the Oregon Film & Video Office, Astoria first showed up in movies in 1908, when *The Fisherman's Bride* was filmed here. It took a while for Hollywood to come calling, but in 1984 Ste- ven Spielberg used Astoria and some of the surrounding towns as the setting for the cult classic, *The Goonies*, a film about what happens to a bunch of kids who find a treasure map. Since then movie crews have returned often to film scenes for hits such as *Short Circuit, Free Willy I* and *II* , *Kindergarten Cop, Teenage Mutant Ninja Turtles III, Into the Wild* and many other films.

A free audio tour and map called "The Reel Astoria" includes descriptions and locations of a dozen local spots that have had star- ring film roles, including the school where Arnold Schwarzenegger posed as a teacher in *Kindergarten Cop.* To download the audio tour and map visit www.oldoregon.com.

Oregon's Banana Belt
Brookings

Located just north of the California border and blessed with the mild-est climate on the Oregon coast, Brookings is known as the state's banana belt. But they don't grow bananas here; they grow lilies. More than 90 percent of the nation's Easter lilies are grown in and around Brookings, earning it the title of Easter Lily Capital of the World. Ironically, the lily fields are not allowed to go to bloom. Each year most all the bulbs are harvested and shipped to greenhouses in the Midwest where the bulbs are tricked into blooming around Easter instead of at their natural blooming time in July. In fact, prior to har-vesting, if a plant looks like it's getting ready to bloom, the blossom

Scenes for *The Goonies* were filmed in this jail.
Astoria-Warrenton Chamber of Commerce

is plucked from the plant; literally nipped in the bud.

As important as lilies are today to the area's economy, the large trumpet-shaped flowers weren't always a popular crop. Prior to 1941 most Easter lilies in the United States came from Japan. But during World War II, when the bulbs could no longer be imported, prices for lily bulbs skyrocketed. All of a sudden growing lilies domestically seemed very appealing.

The unique combination of climate, water, and soil made the Brookings area an ideal spot for this crop, and the lily-perfect conditions allowed local farmers to excel in the market. Today more than eleven million Easter lily bulbs are shipped from this region each year, and Easter lilies represent the country's fourth-largest crop in the potted plant market, right behind poinsettias, mums, and azaleas.

Brookings is about 6 miles north of the California border on US 101.

WWII Bomb Site

Brookings

Most folks know the story of how the Japanese bombed Pearl Harbor on the morning of December 7, 1941. Few people know, however, that the first bombing of the U.S. mainland occurred in Oregon nine months later.

On September 9, 1942, a seaplane launched from an Imperial Japanese Navy submarine dropped incendiary bombs on a heavily wooded section of Mount Emily, 16 miles east of Brookings. No real harm was done: Three of the bombs were duds, and the fourth started a small blaze that was quickly put out. But folks were shaken up, and soon military and government officials showed up to investigate.

In 1962, in the spirit of international relations and friendship and as part of an effort to promote the town, the local Jaycees tracked down and invited the pilot of that seaplane, Chief Flying Officer Nobuo Fujita, to Brookings for the town's annual Azalea Festival. Some local veterans groups were upset by the invitation, but Fujita made the trip.

Nobuo Fujita once tried to bomb Brookings.
Curry Coastal Pilot

All turned out well. During a festival banquet Fujita presented the City of Brookings with his family's 400-year-old samurai sword. "It is in the finest of samurai traditions," Fujita said, "to pledge peace and friendship by submitting the sword to a former enemy." That sword is now on display in the Chetco Community Public Library at 405 Alder Street, 2 blocks east of Chetco Avenue on the south end of Brookings.

Over the years the Brookings-Fujita friendship grew. The former pilot established a fund at the library for the purchase of books about different cultures, sponsored several local high school students as exchange students to Japan, donated Japanese windsocks to be flown during the Azalea Festival, and made a ceremonial visit to the bomb site to say prayers and plant a redwood tree. And on the day before Fujita died, at age eighty-six, a representative of the Brookings City Council delivered an official document proclaiming the former airman an honorary citizen of Brookings.

★ ★

Today the bombing is commemorated with a plaque on the 2-mile Mount Emily Bombsite Trail, which is located 18 miles east of Brookings. From US 101 take County Road 808 (South Bank Road) to Forest Service Road 1205 (Mount Emily Road). The trip includes about 10 miles of gravel road. The 1-mile trail is located off FSR 1205 after spur road number 260.

Call Your Mummy
Cannon Beach

If you're heading toward Cannon Beach late at night, be sure to keep your car doors locked. Otherwise you may end up giving a ride to the unwanted hitchhiker the locals refer to as the Bandage Man of Cannon Beach.

Wrapped completely in, yup, bandages, this bloody apparition is supposedly the ghost of a logger who was cut into pieces in a sawmill accident many years ago. The story around here is that he smells of rotting flesh and can easily jump into the back of pickup trucks and open-topped cars passing between Cannon Beach and the dark stretch of road where US 26 intersects with US 101.

Filmed Here

Haystack Rock Beach, Ecola State Park, and other spots in and around Cannon Beach were used as locations for scenes in several well-known movies, including *The Goonies* (1985); *Kindergarten Cop* (1990), with Arnold Schwarzenegger; *Free Willy* (1993); and *Point Break* (1991), with Patrick Swayze and Keanu Reeves.

Over the years there have been occasional reports of the Bandage Man mysteriously showing up in the backseats of sedans, station wagons, and sports cars—even in vehicles with all their doors locked and all their windows rolled up tight. And while the Bandage Man always seems to conveniently vanish before a frightened driver steers his vehicle into town, there's usually a bit of bloody cloth left behind as a souvenir.

Rubber Ducks and Chow Mein Noodles
Cannon Beach

High tides, strong currents, and stormy northwest weather are the beachcomber's best friends: that's when the best treasures get washed up onto beaches. Seashells, curiously shaped driftwood, and pieces of colored glass worn smooth by the tumble of the waves are common finds, but sometimes the tides roll back to reveal more unusual items.

That's what happened on Oregon's north coast in 1991 when folks woke up to find thousands of brand new Nike sneakers in among the seashells. The shoes weren't castoffs from underwater joggers: A year earlier, a ship bound for Asia with a cargo of 80,000 Nike shoes had lost its load, and the Japanese current had finally brought the sneakers of all sizes to the beaches of Clatsop County. Enterprising locals gathered up what they could and eventually set up informal shoe-swapping parties so folks could try to match single sneakers with their soggy-but-still-wearable sole mates.

It turns out that merchandise tides aren't all that rare. High seas send thousands of shipping containers overboard each year, and oceanographers studying ocean currents have learned a great deal from tracking all that lost stuff as it makes its way to the beaches. Some experts can even predict what will show up where and when. In recent years, for example, alerts have gone out about the impending arrival of a flotilla of rubber duckies, millions of Lego pieces, thousands of cans of chow mein noodles, and several more containers of lost Nike sneakers.

★ ★

Here Today, Gone Today
Cannon Beach

In March 1964 a tsunami generated by an earthquake in Alaska hit the little coastal town of Cannon Beach. The rush of water caused a great deal of local property damage and washed out the bridge linking the town to the highway. Plans for a new bridge further inland were announced, but locals worried that the tiny town would be bypassed and forgotten by tourists on their coastal vacations.

All aboard the Potty Train.
George Vetter/Cannon-Beach.Net

★ ★

In his book *Cannon Beach, A Place by the Sea*, Terence O'Donnell describes several failed "schemes" hatched by locals to lure folks to town. One involved the appearance of a "headless horseman" in downtown Cannon Beach each Sunday at noon. Another less scary and even less successful plan called for pointing giant spotlights at Haystack Rock, the town's beachfront behemoth that is also the world's third-largest monolith. Unfortunately, on the first night the monster lights were turned on, waves of frightened seabirds rose up and flew away over the town. The bird poop they dropped on their way out ensured that the light show was a one-night-only event.

But then another ocean-induced phenomenon hit the beaches: In July 1965 Cannon Beach experienced the lowest tides of the century. While locals looked forward to seeing areas of the beach never seen before, town boosters looked forward to welcoming curious out-of-towners. Everyone joined forces and set about organizing the town's first sand castle building contest.

Today Cannon Beach holds the title for first and oldest sand castle contest in the continental United States. Each June during Sand Castle Day, thousands of folks hit the beach to create sensational sand creations or to just watch amateur and professional artists rushing around to build imaginative, elaborate, and very temporary sculptures that will be washed away in the afternoon tide.

The rules are simple: Builders may only use the sand in their allotted 20-by-20-foot plot and may only add natural objects from the beach such as seaweed, driftwood, and shells. Tools are allowed and can be anything from specially created wooden forms to the traditional, brightly-colored, kid-size beach pails and shovels. And the sand subjects can be anything, within reason: The contest rules emphasize that because "this is a wholesome, family-fun time, risqué ideas are unacceptable."

Cannon Beach is 80 miles west of Portland. To get there take US 26 to US 101 S. For more information on Sand Castle Day, call (503) 436-2623 or visit www.cannon-beach.org.

Castles in the Sand

Cannon Beach isn't the only Oregon town that pits people with pails and shovels against the impending tide. Lincoln City holds its annual Sand Castle Contest the first or second Saturday of each August (depending on the tides) at Fifty-first Street, on the south end of town. And in Port Orford the Sandcastle Building Contest is just one of several competitions (don't miss the knot-tying contest or the dingy races) held during the Port Orford Jubilee, which takes place during the July Fourth holiday.

For more information about the Lincoln City Sand Castle Contest, call (541) 996-1274 or visit www.oregoncoast.org. For the Port Orford Jubilee and Sandcastle Building Contest, call (541) 332-4106 or visit www.discoverportorford.com.

Check In, Never Check Out
Cannon Beach

Standing 133 feet above sea level on an island of solid basalt, the 62-foot-high Tillamook Rock Lighthouse sits more than a mile offshore from Tillamook Head. Building a lighthouse out there in 1880 was clearly no small feat: During construction the project foreman drowned, and workmen had to endure raging seas that often sent waves crashing across the site. Living up to its nickname of "Terrible Tilly," the lighthouse was no piece of cake to operate either: The waters in this area are among the roughest in the world, and lighthouse keepers often went months without getting deliveries of needed provisions.

Still, Oregon's northernmost lighthouse operated for more than three-quarters of a century before modern navigational tools and high maintenance costs put the station out of business. On

No place for the living or the dead.
U.S. Coast Guard

September 1, 1957, the light was put out, and the structure was sold to a private owner.

In 1980 the lighthouse was sold again. This time to real estate developers who turned Terrible Tilly into a columbarium, or "cemetery at sea." Her windows and ports were cemented over, metal plates replaced the glass panes in the lantern, and a few thousand spaces were created to hold urns containing human ashes. Resting spots at the Eternity at Sea Columbarium were put on the market for prices ranging from $1,000 to $5,000, depending on the "view."

The site was never open to the (living) public, and only a few dozen urns were ever placed in the lighthouse. And it turned out that the business of collecting cash for stashing human remains in an old lighthouse wasn't that easy: In 2005 the owners lost their license to operate the columbarium due to poor record keeping and improper care and storage of the urns.

★ ★

Today the lighthouse remains on the National Register of Historic Places but no new reservations for long-term guests are being taken. Still, on a clear day you can see the eerie-looking lighthouse from Ecola State Park, which is probably as close as you'd really want to get to Terrible Tilly anyway.

Ecola State Park is off US 101, 2 miles north of Cannon Beach. For more information about the lighthouse, go to www.worldlights.com. For park information visit www.oregonstateparks.org/park_188.php.

Squeeze In If You Can

Depoe Bay

Located on the stretch of central Oregon's coastal highway known as the "Twenty Miracle Miles," Depoe Bay is a former commercial fishing town that now draws whale-watchers, sportfishing enthusiasts, and tourists who come to see what the *Guinness Book of World Records* has declared to be the world's smallest navigable natural harbor.

The six-acre port is located just east of the concrete arches of the Depoe Bay Bridge and is only 750 feet long, 390 feet wide, and 8 feet deep at low tide. The tiny harbor also has a tiny entrance: a narrow slot in the basalt cliffs that can only accommodate boats up to 50 feet in length. So it's not unusual to see tourists gathered to watch vessels try to make their way to and from the sea, an activity known locally as "shooting the hole."

Depoe Bay is also known as the Whale Watching Capital of Oregon, in honor of the resident pod of gray whales that stays nearby practically year-round. Those whales can often be spotted from observation spots onshore and from the many whale-watching charters that head out from the harbor. Landlubbers—and kids—will also enjoy visiting the large whale statue made out of spray-foam insulation at Whale Park, on the north end of the town's seawall.

The natural (and spray foam) wonders don't stop there. Depoe Bay also has two "spouting horns." Waves running beneath lava beds

Oregon boasts the world's smallest navigable natural harbor.
AZ Ray's; www.azrays photoart.com

along the ocean shore build up pressure and, during certain tidal conditions, spout water out of natural blowholes as high as 60 feet in the air. The effect is best during stormy weather when the sea is especially turbulent.

Depoe Bay is located on US 101, 12 miles north of Newport. For more information contact the Depoe Bay Chamber of Commerce at (541) 765-2889 or visit www.depoebaychamber.org.

★ ★

Filmed Here

In the movie version of Ken Kesey's *One Flew Over the Cuckoo's Nest*, Jack Nicholson's character, Randle McMurphy, and a crew of fellow mental patient escapees headed out on a charter boat from Depoe Bay for a day of salmon fishing.

A Whale of a Time

Florence

It was really big, definitely dead, and incredibly smelly. And on November 12, 1970, the 45-foot, eight-ton dead sperm whale that had washed up on the beach near Florence was getting smellier by the minute.

That's when the Oregon State Highway Division stepped in.

But getting rid of the slimy, stinky thing wasn't easy. If they buried the whale, it might get uncovered by the tides. And no one wanted to get in there, cut it up, and then bury it because it was too smelly. Burning it didn't seem like a good option either.

So after consulting with experts at the Navy, the Highway Division decided the best thing to do was to put a half ton of dynamite inside the beached whale and blow the dang thing up. The small pieces left behind in the water, they confidently announced, would provide a free dinner for the seagulls and crabs.

But something went terribly wrong. The explosion—which was caught on tape by a Portland television station—was impressive but not strong enough to destroy the entire carcass. Huge pieces of the whale were sent flying. Not toward the water as planned, but instead right toward the crowds of onlookers up on the dunes, who were forced to run for cover as small pieces of stinky whale flesh fell from the sky. Miraculously, no one was seriously hurt, though one car parked a quarter-mile away did get crushed by a chunk of falling blubber.

Highway Division staff later buried what was left of the whale, but they haven't been able to bury the story. The video of the news report on the exploding whale has become collectible film footage, and once the Internet took hold, the film became a much-downloaded classic. Then, in 1990, Pulitzer Prize–winning writer Dave Barry came upon the exploding whale footage and wrote a column about it, thinking it was a new occurrence. His jokes about the blubber flub-up showed up in hundreds of other papers that also reported the whale explosion as a fresh event.

Officials at the Oregon State Highway Division, now the Oregon Department of Transportation, had to spend hours setting the record straight. But in reliving the stinky, decades-old event, they were able to reassure the public that something had been learned from the 1970 blubber-blast. When a pod of forty-one dead sperm whales washed ashore on the beach in 1979, officials from the state parks department burned and buried the carcasses. Nowadays dead whales are usually towed out to sea.

The now classic 1970 TV news report of the exploding whale, including falling blubber, is available at www.theexplodingwhale.com and other Web sites.

Carnivorous Cobra Lilies
Florence

The California pitcher plant looks innocent enough. Even its botanical name, *Darlingtonia californica*, sounds, well, darling and sort of innocent. But you get a hint of the plant's real nature once you learn where it grows—in wet meadows and bogs—and when you learn its common name—cobra lily.

Rare and strange-looking, the cobra lily is the only member of the pitcher family to make its home in Oregon. With yellowish-green, cobra-like hoods on top of hollow tubes that can grow up to 20

★ ★

Don't get too close. These plants eat meat!
Thor Steen

inches long, the plants are intriguing to look at—that is, if you're a
human. Insects that get a little too close run the risk of becoming
dinner. A hidden opening behind the leaves around the plant's hood
leads to an opening in the stalk. Nectar inside that hidden opening
attracts insects, and once inside, well, there's no turning back. A
visiting insect will get confused by a series of fake exits and eventually drop into the lower part of the tube where it will get trapped
by downward-pointed hairs and then fall into a pool of water at the
bottom of the stalk. Death comes by way of bacteria in the water
that decompose the insect and transform what's left into nitrogen
that is then absorbed by the plant. Yum!

Want to see the darling cobra lily in action? Stop by the Darlingtonia State Natural Site, just off US 101, north of the town of Florence.
The eighteen-acre botanical park sits on a peat bog that's home
to an unusual concentration of carnivorous cobra lilies and is the
only Oregon state park dedicated to the protection of a single plant

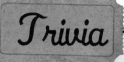

Florence Facts

- Florence sits at the exact midpoint of the Oregon coast.

- The beach behind Florence is the starting point of a 50-mile stretch of sand dunes known as the Oregon Dunes National Recreation Area. The dunes reach to Coos Bay and are the largest expanse of sand dunes in the country.

- Known as the "City of Rhododendrons," Florence has held a Rhododendron Festival every year since 1908.

species. A boardwalk with interpretive signs leads out to the pitcher-plant preserve, past more mild-mannered scenery that includes rhododendron and shore pine.

For more information on the park, call (800) 551-6949 or visit www.oregonstateparks.org/park_115.php.

Haunted Lighthouse
Florence

The 56-foot-tall historic Heceta Head Lighthouse sits 205 feet above the ocean at Heceta Head State Park. It's said to be one of the most visited and most photographed lighthouses in the country, but only some of the people who stay overnight at the light keeper assistants' house next door get to meet Rue, the resident ghost.

But first the lighthouse: Built between 1892 and 1894 with local lumber, cement, and masonry from San Francisco, and tons of rocks from the Clackamas River in Oregon City, the lighthouse has a "first order" Fresnel lens that can be seen 21 miles out to sea. It is the brightest light on the Oregon coast.

If you see Rue, the resident ghost, be sure to wave.

For years light keepers needed to be on hand to make sure that the light flashed every minute from sunset to sunrise. That meant hauling coal oil up the tower to feed the kerosene lamplight that was magnified and beamed out to sea. Every four hours the light keepers also had to hand crank the weighted clockworks that turned the lamp. Technology eventually put the light keepers out of business: In 1934 the lightbulb replaced the oil lamp, and in 1963 the lighthouse became automated.

When they were on duty, though, the lighthouse keepers lived on-site in two buildings—one for the head keeper and another for two assistants. Today one building, the Queen Anne–style light keeper assistants' house, remains standing. Known now as Heceta House, it operates as a popular bed-and-breakfast and has been called one of the ten most haunted houses in the United States.

Rue, the resident ghost, is believed to be the mother of a young girl who fell off the cliffs and died. She's made her presence known over the years with all sorts of unexplained, mysterious occurrences such as unidentified screams, objects that move or go missing, and face-to-face encounters between guests and a shadowy woman with silver hair and a long dark dress.

Rue has also been credited with sweeping up broken glass and, in general, being helpful and nonthreatening. Still, guests who head outdoors late to bask in the night sky from the base of the lighthouse tower are reminded to bring flashlights with extra batteries, to count their companions and to wave to the gray-haired lady looking down from the attic window.

The Heceta Head Lighthouse State Scenic Viewpoint and the park at the cove below the lighthouse are operated by the Oregon State Parks Department. Scheduled tours of the lighthouse and the interpretive center on the first floor of the Heceta House are available during the summer and by appointment year-round. Occasional night tours (for the very brave) are offered throughout the year as well.

Heceta Head Lighthouse is located on US 101, 13 miles north of

★ ★

Don't Leave Yet

Trails around Heceta Head lead to various beach and wildlife-viewing areas. From here you can see wildlife refuge islands set aside as nesting areas for puffins, cormorants, gulls, and other birds. Sea lions and whales traveling to and from Alaska and Baja California can often be seen from the beach and lighthouse. May is an especially good time to see migrating mother whales with their calves traveling close to the shore.

Florence and 11 miles south of Yachats. There is a day-use fee for the park. For more information about the Heceta Head Lighthouse State Scenic Viewpoint, call (541) 547-3416 or visit www.oregonstateparks .org/park_124.php. For information about the interpretive center and the bed-and-breakfast in the Heceta House next door, call (866) 547-3696 or go to www.hecetalighthouse.com.

See the Sea Cave
Florence

The *Guinness Book of World Records* has declared the twelve-story-high, football-field-length Sea Lion Caves to be the World's Largest Sea Cave. Formed from basalt about twenty-five million years ago and discovered in 1880 by William Cox (who was once trapped inside the cave for several days), the caves are now a popular tourist spot in part because they're the year-round home of a herd of about 200 Steller sea lions.

Visiting the caves is an adventure unto itself. A walkway leads across a bluff to an elevator that travels more than 200 feet down into the caves. From there visitors can marvel at the caves and explore a small museum featuring the skeleton of a 7-foot-long,

* *

Make sure you see the sea lion caves near Florence.

three-year-old female Stellar sea lion that was found near Newport with a fatal gunshot wound.

By far, though, the main attractions here are the live and often very loudmouthed sea lions that congregate inside the caves in the fall and winter and on a sunny ledge just outside the caves during the warmer months. It's especially fun to visit in late spring and summer, when dozens of sea lion pups are born.

The Sea Lion Caves are open year-round at 91560 US 101, 11 miles north of Florence and 38 miles south of Newport. There is an admission fee for the elevator ride, but it's possible to see the sea lions, Heceta Head Lighthouse, seabirds, and the occasional whale for free from ledges nearby. For more information call (541) 547-3111 or go to www.sealioncaves.com.

Don't forget to bring binoculars, a jacket (the caves are cool even in summer), and a camera. And don't say you weren't warned about the smell.

★ ★

Catch anything?

Hebo

Long before this giant fishing rod came to rest on top of the Nestucca Valley Sporting Goods store in Hebo, it was familiar to some locals as a prize-winning parade float that came with its own fresh-from-the-sea mermaid. But before it was a float or a fishing rod it was a discarded light pole that Phil Jacobs rescued from a parking lot.

Jacobs got hooked on the idea of turning that old light pole into a giant rod and reel. He couldn't do it alone, though, so he lured a bunch of his friends in on the project. One buddy machined the handle and fabricated the guides. Others created, assembled, and wrapped assorted parts. A reel was fashioned out of a big electrical spool; an ocean float became a bobber; and a special bracket was designed to allow the rod to be raised and lowered on a flatbed trailer. When someone floated the idea of having a live mermaid on the end of the line, they knew they had a winner. The float became a

This giant fishing rod definitely reels 'em in.
Original Nestucca Valley Sporting Goods; Chuck Fahrni

regular in many local parades and, before it was retired, the rod had won a boatload of trophies, including first place in the 1992 Garibaldi Maritime parade.

In 2006 Pat and Laurie Gefre learned that the pole was still around and stored in a local barn. They bought it, fixed it up, and had it hoisted to the top of their store. Now when visitors stop by and ask just what kind of fish this unique rod was designed to catch, the Gefres willingly take the bait and answer, "Customers!"

To see the big fishing reel, drive by the Nestucca Valley Sporting Goods in Hebo, which is south of Tillamook at the junction of US 101 and US 22. For more information call (503) 392-4269 or see www .nestuccariveroutfitters.com.

Named for Abe

Lincoln City

What happens when towns are too tiny?

Merging is one option. And in the mid-1950s that's what five towns on the Oregon coast agreed to do. But what the citizens in Cutler City, Taft, Delake, Oceanlake, and Nelscott could not agree on was which town's name would survive. So an entirely new name for the proposed city was called for.

More than 300 suggestions poured in. Adults favored the name Lincoln City, in part because in 1849 Abraham Lincoln had been offered the position of governor of the Oregon Territory. (He declined.) Area schoolchildren were campaigning for the more fun-sounding Surfland. But that name was ultimately rejected as being too "honky-tonk."

Today Lincoln City is a thriving tourist town with art galleries, fine restaurants, and, some say, a good measure of honky-tonk attractions. The town also has a 14-foot bronze statue of Abraham Lincoln, titled *On the Circuit*, that was given to the city in 1964 on the condition that it keep the Lincoln City name—and keep the Lincoln statue facing west.

He could have been governor of the Oregon Territory.
Sandy Pfaff, Lincoln City Convention and Visitor Bureau

A while back, though, the statue was moved, and it (temporarily, city officials insist), faces north, 2 blocks east of US 101 at Northeast Twenty-first Street and Port Avenue.

First Honeymooners on the Oregon Coast
Lincoln City

These days, newlyweds might spend their honeymoon in Hawaii or Tahiti, or perhaps rent a cute little cottage at the beach.

It turns out that the sea and sand have been beckoning honey-mooners to the Oregon coast long before there were motels, exotic bridal suites, or cozy seaside cottages for let. In fact, Lincoln City claims to be the destination for the first honeymooners on the entire Oregon coast.

As the story goes, on August 14, 1837, Reverend Jason Lee and Cyrus Shephard traveled by horseback with their brides from the Willamette Valley down the Salmon River Trail to the Oregon coast, arriving in the Lincoln City area on August 18. The group set up camp by a small grove of evergreens and, over the next week, played in the surf, ate their fill of clams and fish, and "cured themselves of malaria and evangelized the Salmon River Indians."

Sounds awfully romantic, doesn't it?

Redhead Roundup
Lincoln City

In the 1930s and again in the 1940s after WWII, towns along the Oregon coast waged hot competition for tourists and businesses. Regattas, fishing contests, and carnivals were all popular. But certainly one of the more unusual events was the Redhead Roundup in Taft, which is now part of Lincoln City.

According to newspaper accounts of the time, ninety-one redheads registered to participate in the Second Annual Redhead Roundup held on August 14, 1932. Events included boat races, diving exhibitions, and prizes for the largest family of redheads. That contest was won hands down by a family with seven redheads in attendance. The triumphant family told judges that they had one redheaded daughter with a redheaded son of her own, neither of whom could attend that day, and, back home, a red dog and a farm on which they raised Rhode Island red chickens, red hogs, and red cows.

Over the years Taft's Redhead Roundup incorporated a wide variety of events, including log rolling, fly casting, deep-sea fishing, and, in 1935, a bathing beauty contest that, the newspapers noted, had three times as many judges as contestants. These days, many coastal towns lure visitors with kite festivals, beachcombing, whale watching, and other activities of interest to redheads, brunettes, and blondes alike.

★ ★

World's Shortest River?

Lincoln City

There's a long-running debate over whether the World's Shortest River is the D River in Lincoln City or the Roe River in Great Falls, Montana. Each has been measured multiple times, and due to factors such as tides, season, and soil erosion, their lengths have varied from 58 feet to 200 feet. Sick of the unrelenting squabble, the folks at the *Guinness Book of World Records* declared a tie.

Or so they thought. For a while Lincoln City and Great Falls were content to share honors. But then some schoolchildren in Great Falls took up the cause and successfully petitioned to have their river declared the sole shortest.

Don't blink—you'll miss it!
Sandy Pfaff, Lincoln City Convention and Visitor Bureau

★ ✦ ★ ✦ ★ ✦ ★ ✦ ★ ✦ ★ ✦ ★ ✦ ★ ✦ ★ ✦ ★ ✦ ★ ✦ ★ ✦ ★ ✦ ★ ✦ ★ ✦ ★

But that doesn't faze the folks in Lincoln City. In print and in person, pretty much everyone in town still maintains that, at an average of 120 feet, the D River that flows from Devil's Lake into the nearby Pacific Ocean is indeed the World's Shortest River. The D cuts through a windy beach that's been designated an Oregon State Recreation Site and is popular with kite fliers and the home of two annual kite festivals. You can find it on US 101, in the center of Lincoln City. "There's a traffic light there—you can't miss it," insists a fellow at the visitor center.

For more information call the Lincoln City Visitor and Convention Bureau at (800) 452-2151 or visit www.oregoncoast.org.

Eek a Ghost
Lincoln City

Searching for a spirit? The folks in Lincoln City have scads of them and have put together the EEEKO Tour to lead visitors to the spookiest spots. Here's a sampling:

Staff at the Wildflower Grill (4250 Northeast Highway 101) believe a ghost named Matilda regularly opens and closes cabinets, rattles the employee restroom's locked doorknob, and once walked right past one the restaurant's owners before disappearing on a balcony.

It may be a friend of Matilda's who spends his time near the bar at the Spouting Horn Restaurant (110 Southeast Highway 101), just 8 miles down the road in Depoe Bay. "Ralph" has been seen wearing a cook's apron with his "arms crossed, and staring as if to suggest the humans he encountered were intruding on his territory," and employees frequently see him crossing the hallway to the dining room.

At the Devils Lake Fire Station in north Lincoln City (2525 Northwest Highway 101), modern-day volunteers believe the spirit of a former volunteer firefighter, "Bob," spends his time hanging around the first fire truck put into service at the station, which is kept in the back bay. He's often heard walking up and down the stairs during the

Watch for ghost ships on the water.
Sandy Pfaff, Lincoln City Convention & Visitor Bureau

night, and once was found napping on the break room couch before he quickly vanished.

While the "haunted" restaurants are, of course, open to the public, visitors are discouraged from just popping in at the fire station. But all are welcome at Siletz Bay, on the south end of Lincoln City, where a sailing ship washed up onshore about 150 years ago. That vessel may be the source of the ghost ship that's occasionally seen sailing into the bay above the water, and then vanishing into thin air.

And then there's the creature said to inhabit the 680-acre freshwater lake on the northeast side of Lincoln City. The lake empties into the ocean through the 120-foot D River and was known

★ ★

centuries ago as Indian Bay. Legend has it that many Siletz Indians vanished into its waters when pulled from their vessels by giant tentacles reaching up from below. So watch your step.

More information about these and other spooky spots on the EEEKO Tour is available at the Lincoln City Visitor and Convention Bureau offices at 801 Southwest Highway 101 in Lincoln City, at (800) 452-2151, and at www.oregoncoast.org.

None of Your Beeswax
Neahkahnie Mountain

There are two curious and mysterious legends surrounding shipwrecks on the beach near Neahkahnie Mountain, which juts 1,600 feet above the beach just north of Manzanita. One involves buried treasure, the other beeswax.

First, the treasure: According to coastal lore that reaches back to the Clatsop Indians who originally lived in this area, a landing party from a ship that either anchored offshore of Neahkahnie Mountain or wrecked on the beach below was seen trying to secretly bury a "black box" on the mountain. They supposedly marked the spot of what was certainly buried treasure with a specially inscribed rock.

To this day, though, no sign of the treasure has been found, and some say that's due in no small part to the hard work of the vigilant ghost said to be guarding the booty. Want to try to find the treasure? Mysterious inscribed rocks that may be some sort of map to the treasure were found on the mountain and are now on display in Tillamook at the Tillamook County Pioneer Museum.

And what about the beeswax? When Lewis and Clark showed up here, beeswax was among the items being traded by local tribes. And early settlers to the area encountered chunks of beeswax on the beach that sometimes weighed up to 200 pounds. For a long time it was assumed paraffin was a naturally occurring substance here, but that theory melted away when cakes of wax stamped with the monogram of the Catholic Church showed up. Most likely the beeswax came from shipwrecked Spanish galleons lost at sea during supply runs to Catholic missions in the mid-to-late 1700s. Some of that beeswax is on display at the Tillamook County Pioneer Museum as well.

Think you can find that lost treasure? There are several hikes you can take on Neahkahnie Mountain. One access point is from US 101 just south of Oswald West State Park on the east side of the highway, between mileposts forty-one and forty-two. The mysterious inscribed rocks and examples of beeswax from the beach can be seen at the Tillamook County Pioneer Museum, located at 2106 Second Street in Tillamook. For hours and directions call (503) 842-4553 or visit www.tcpm.org.

B&B Riverboat

Newport

Is it a riverboat or a hotel?

No need to decide. The *Newport Belle* is both a stern-wheeler riverboat and a bed-and-breakfast. Constructed in 1993 and moored in the Newport Marina, the 97-foot-long *Belle* is a U.S. Coast Guard–registered vessel and, as far as owners Nancy Sims and husband Michael Wilkinson can tell, it's the only B&B riverboat in North America.

Guests who climb aboard this three-deck hotel report being "hooked" once they encounter the cozy indoor salon with wood stove and the aft deck above the paddle wheel that offers the perfect perch for watching the sunset and the boats in the marina. "The *Belle* does rock a bit when the wind blows forcefully," says Sims, "but many guests say that it feels as if they're being gently rocked to sleep." And while all five staterooms have private baths, just like "real" hotels, the *Belle* offers guests an amenity not found at inns on land: Each room comes equipped with two life jackets.

The *Newport Belle* is located in the Newport Marina in Newport. From US 101 in Newport, head south on the Yaquina Bay Bridge. Take the first right and follow the signs to the Newport Marina and

A floating bed-and-breakfast makes for a rocking good time.
Michael Wilkinson

the Hatfield Marine Science Center. At the science center turn left into the large parking lot and go across the lot to the *Newport Belle*, which is moored at H Dock. For more information call (800) 348-1922 or go to www.newportbelle.com.

You Light Up My Life
Newport

To be crowned Miss America these days a young woman must be poised, smart, talented, and lovely. But back in 1891 it surely took belief in the latest newfangled technology to land the title of Miss Electricity.

In the late nineteenth century, folks back east were already well acquainted with the wonders of Thomas Edison and electric light. But in many communities, especially those out west, people were still quite wary. For example, even though the town of Independence,

Miss Electricity 1891 was light on her feet.
Lincoln County Historical Society

Oregon, had installed electricity in 1890, it was deemed safe only for outdoor lighting.

By 1891, however, an Independence opera house decided to install indoor electric lights. To allay local fears, the Electric Light Co. decided to create and crown Miss Electricity. Sixteen-year-old Lulu Miller of Newport got the job.

In her formal portrait, now displayed at Newport's Oregon Coast History Center, Lulu Miller (Nye) seems to be, well, glowing. It could be because she's draped in a string of light bulbs, or "incandescent lamps," jauntily cinched at her waist. Or perhaps because she's sporting a bevy of bulbs on the points of her crown and on her ribbon-festooned scepter.

According to a newspaper account at the time, Miss Electricity was first introduced at a trade carnival being held in the newly wired opera house. "Miss Miller . . . stepped forward and suddenly was enveloped in a flood of light . . . The audience was so enthusiastic that a recall was necessary." Lulu's luminosity, the report continued, was made possible by "copper plates on the stage and in the soles of Miss Miller's shoes [that] caused the electric current to flash through the wires concealed in the folds of her clothing. It was a beautiful sight."

Miss Electricity's portrait is on display at Newport's Oregon Coast History Center at 545 Southwest Ninth Street. Hours vary by season. For more information call (541) 265-7509 or visit www.oregoncoast .history.museum.

Between the Covers
Newport

Like a weekend trip to the beach, an uninterrupted afternoon with a good book can be a relaxing getaway. If that sounds appealing, then imagine heading to the beach and unpacking your bags at a hotel with no radios, televisions, or telephones but plenty of book-filled guest rooms designed to evoke the work of famous authors.

Toothpick Bridge

In addition to the portrait of Miss Electricity 1891, the Oregon Coast History Center displays an ingenious foghorn made from an old tuba and a set of bellows, an unusual Native American beaded skirt with a fringe of thimbles, and a toothpick model of the arched Yaquina Bay Bridge that spans Yaquina Bay, just south of Newport.

Completed in 1936, the bridge (not the toothpick model) was the last link on the Oregon Coast Highway. It took more than two years to build, at a cost of about $1.3 million. Using a design adapted from Oregon State Highway Division blueprints, local civic groups built the toothpick model in 142 hours using six boxes of toothpicks and about a quart of glue. Total cost: $5.

Yaquina Bay Bridge—the original version.
Oregon Department of Transportation

Yaquina Bay Bridge—the toothpick version.
Lincoln County Historical Society

You can see the Yaquina Bay Bridge at the south end of Newport, on US 101. The toothpick model of the bridge is part of the
Bridges of Lincoln County display in Newport's Oregon Coast History Center. Call (541) 265-7509 or visit www.oregoncoast.history
.museum.

That's what Goody Cable and her good friend Sally Ford had in mind when they rescued a dilapidated former beach resort on a 45-foot bluff above the ocean in Newport. They recruited handy, book-loving friends and transformed the circa 1912 Cliff House into a bed-and-breakfast for book lovers.

For starters, they named the place the Sylvia Beach Hotel, in honor of the woman who owned the Shakespeare and Co. bookstore in Paris during the 1920s and '30s. Then they made each of the twenty guest rooms into a sort-of shrine to a different author and filled each room with decorations and special touches unique to that author and his or her work.

For example, the Ernest Hemingway room has an antelope head on the wall. The Edgar Allan Poe room has a pendulum over the bed, a red velvet comforter, and a taxidermied raven on the desk and is, according to the desk clerk, a favorite with honeymooners.

The Dr. Seuss room is painted in bright primary colors with a *Cat in the Hat* mural on the wall and a rack filled with fun hats. The E. B. White room has a web hanging from the ceiling and framed *New Yorker* covers on the wall. There's also a clue-filled room honoring Agatha Christie and rooms named for Colette, Mark Twain, Alice Walker, Emily Dickinson, F. Scott Fitzgerald, and Herman Melville, among others.

While the twenty rooms are named for noted authors, none of them are numbered or, for that matter, plainly marked. Instead there are words, pictures, or clues. For example, "Stell-a" is written on the door to the Tennessee Williams room. That seems somewhat straightforward. But what about that knotted rope on the Mark Twain room door? It seems "Mark Twain" was a term used on the Mississippi River to refer to the 12-foot, or 2 fathoms, mark on a depth-measuring knotted rope line, the safe depth for a steamboat.

Need help deciphering the other clues on the doors? There's a well-stocked library here and a small restaurant called Tables of Content where the conversation leans toward, you guessed it, great books.

★ ★

The Sylvia Beach Hotel is located several blocks off US 101, at 267 Northwest Cliff Street in Newport. For more information call (541) 265-5428 or visit www.sylviabeachhotel.com.

Myrtlewood Money
North Bend

Travelers on the southern Oregon coast will surely notice the lovely myrtlewood trees that grow here. A member of the laurel family, this dense, broad-leaved evergreen has intricately grained, multihued wood that is used to make everything from bowls and platters to toys, furniture, and sculpture. And while you can pay a pretty penny for some special myrtlewood pieces, there was a period during the Great Depression when the town of North Bend used the wood itself as currency.

In 1933 North Bend's only bank abruptly closed, leaving residents and the city government without access to their funds. Finding themselves with a payroll to make and plenty of bills to pay, city officials put their heads together, called a city council meeting, and passed an ordinance authorizing the issuance of special Depression-era money made from local myrtlewood. In short order first $1,000 and then a second $1,000 worth of locally made tokens were issued, valued at 25 cents to $10. The plan for the new currency was announced in the local paper:

> The money will go into circulation at once in payment of salaries of employees of the city. They in turn will pass it out to merchants for merchandise or purchases of whatsoever nature, and the merchant will pass it out to his employees. Those who receive the money through their regular channels of business should make an effort to keep the money in circulation, instead of storing some away. In this manner, the fullest possible benefit may be obtained.

Many coins entered circulation, but a good many were snapped up by collectors, including the Chase Manhattan Bank of New York, which sent a letter informing the city that it was adding a full set of myrtlewood money to the bank's own coin collection.

This myrtlewood money is still legal tender.
Coos Historical and Maritime Museum

The bank in North Bend did eventually reopen, and the city of North Bend was able to offer cash redemptions to anyone who showed up with the wood tokens. But not everyone turned in their tokens, and because the special money had no expiration date, it would technically still be honored in town today.

Proof to some that, once in a while, money really does grow on trees.

Dynamite Dino-Site
Port Orford

Ernie Nelson was one of those kids who loved dinosaurs. As a grown-up he was an amateur paleontologist who dreamed of building a park filled with his favorite prehistoric creatures. So in the early 1950s, long before anyone ever thought about a place called Jurassic

He won't bite.
Jay Stoler

★ ★

Park, Nelson and his wife set off along the Oregon coast in search of a potential dino-site.

They found a spot in the Port Orford rain forest that had plenty of ferns, moss-covered trees, and lots of mud and muck. Just the sort of primordial landscape, Nelson thought, where dinosaurs and other early reptiles may have roamed. And in 1953, after consulting dinosaur experts to ensure that his creations were scientifically correct, a fifty-year-old Nelson opened his Prehistoric Gardens to the public. Back then he had two giant homemade dinosaurs in residence.

After that, it seems, Nelson just kept going. By the time he died, in 1999, twenty-three of his dinosaurs and prehistoric creatures—some more than 40 feet tall—were planted along the paths in the garden. They may be toothsome, feathered, armored, spotted, or a little bit goofy-looking, but with their often unusual and offbeat paint jobs, it's impossible to miss even the baby dinosaurs that appear to have just hatched from their eggs.

The Prehistoric Gardens are open daily year-round and are located about 12 miles south of Port Orford at 36848 US 101 South. Admission is charged. For more information call (541) 332-4463.

Myrtlewood Mania

The largest myrtlewood tree in Oregon sits in a myrtle grove at the end of the quarter-mile-long Myrtle Tree Trail. The mega-myrtlewood has a canopy about 70 feet wide, is about 88 feet tall, and has a circumference of 42 feet.

To get to the Myrtle Tree Trail, from US 101 at Gold Beach, drive east on Jerry's Flat Road toward Agness for about 9.5 miles. Turn left on Forest Service Road 3310, cross the bridge, and turn right on Silver Creek Road (Forest Service Road 3533). Watch for the trail signs.

Missing Meteorite
Port Orford

While four meteorites (so far) have been recovered in Oregon, there are rumors of several others that have been found and then somehow lost. Among the most curious missing meteorites is the space rock that supposedly fell to earth around Port Orford.

Tantalizing tales of this meteorite began in 1851 when geologist Dr. John Evans was out and about Oregon gathering rocks, fossils, and soil samples as part of a survey project for the government. On that trek Evans says he encountered the tip of what he estimated to be a two-ton rock protruding from the ground. He dutifully chipped off a small sample that, when finally analyzed in 1859, turned out to be from a rare and very valuable pallasite meteorite. Up until then the largest pallasite sample on record was a mere 1,500 pounds, so folks were pretty excited to hear the tale of the two-ton behemoth encountered by Evans.

Plans were under way for Evans and a team of experts to head back to Oregon to find and retrieve the meteorite. Unfortunately, the Civil War broke out, and their plans were put on hold. And shortly thereafter, Dr. Evans died. Sadly for the meteor hunters, Evans had not yet completed the map to the meteorite.

No map. No meteorite. And for a long time, no interest. But meteorite mania heated up again when Dr. Evans's journal surfaced in 1917, containing notes about the general location of the meteorite, including this passage: "Approximately forty miles from Port Orford on the top of Bald Mountain. The sample in question is removed from a partially buried rock on a western-facing grassy slope otherwise free from any other protrusions."

Two search parties from the Smithsonian Institution, sent in 1929 and 1939, couldn't find the meteorite. To this day, no one else has either. And that has led some to believe that the Port Orford meteorite may have been a hoax from the start.

Or perhaps it's still out there.

★ ★

Trivia

Port Orford Factoids

- Port Orford is the oldest town site on the Oregon coast.

- Port Orford is the most westerly incorporated city in the contiguous forty-eight states.

- Port Orford's Cape Blanco Lighthouse is the oldest continually operating lighthouse on the Oregon coast and among the first few on the entire West Coast.

- Port Orford claims to have the shortest state highway. Highway 251 is only 0.7 mile. Locals call it Coast Guard Hill Road, as it leads to an old coast guard station that is now a historical museum and state park.

- The dolly dock at the port of Port Orford is among only a handful of dolly docks in the world. Fishing vessels are hoisted up onto the deck or lowered into the water. When not in use, the boats rest in trailers on the dock.

Chain Saw Savvy
Reedsport

What's the sound of fifty chain saws sawing?

You don't want to know. And, luckily, you don't have to: Free earplugs are handed out to everyone who attends the Oregon Divisional Chainsaw Sculpting Championships in Reedsport.

Held each year over Father's Day weekend, the championship pits chain saw artists from around the world in a seventeen-hour sawdust-and-woodchip-filled carving contest. Armed with chain saws and plenty of skill and imagination, contestants race to transform 8- to

10-foot-tall Sitka spruce logs into award-winning works of art. Along the way there are time-outs for daily "quick-carve" events.

It's hard to imagine how anyone can just look at a chunk of wood and coax a delicate work of art from it with only a loud, obnoxious, destructive piece of power equipment as their carving tool. But chain saw artists do just that, creating everything from realistic-looking animals to intricate scenes with multiple characters. It's definitely an activity that's moved way beyond a funky redneck hobby into the realms of fine art.

The Chainsaw Sculpting Championships are held on the waterfront in downtown Reedsport, which is about 22 miles south of Florence on US 101. For more information call the Reedsport Chamber of Commerce at (800) 247-2155 or visit www.odcsc.com.

You just never know what you'll find inside a log.
Ed Malone

★ ★

Royal Crown Competitors

Seaside

When is really big not big enough? When there are titles and pride involved, of course. And that's what was at the root of the debate over which tree was bigger: the giant Sitka spruce tree in Seaside or the huge Sitka spruce in Washington State.

Until 1987 the Sitka spruce in Seaside was the undisputed king of the forest. But then a tree hunter in Washington measured a Sitka spruce on the eastern shore of Lake Quinault and sent his findings to the folks at American Forests, a nonprofit group that publishes the *National Register of Big Trees*.

After that, there was an all-out Sitka Spruce Slug-Out.

Oregon's Sitka spruce was 204 feet tall. Washington's rose "only" 191 feet above the forest floor. So declaring a winner should have been simple, right?

Well, not exactly.

When it comes to measuring trees, height isn't the only thing that matters. In the world of trees, it turns out that other factors matter, too.

American Forests determines champion trees with a straightforward equation that gives points for a tree's vertical height, its trunk circumference, and its crown spread. New trees may dethrone registered champions if they have more overall points, but when two trees have scores within five points of each other, they're listed as co-champions.

In 1987 tree experts from Washington and Oregon measured the two "largest" Sitka spruces once and for all. Or so they thought. Oregon's Sitka spruce tallied up 856 points. Washington's spruce tipped the scales at 883 points.

So the winner was Washington, right?

Well, not exactly.

Rather than declare a new champion, the folks at American Forests decided that with trees this big in the top ten, it's not worth

The Seaside spruce could withstand controversy
but not, it seems, lightning storms.
Peter Auv

quibbling over a few points. So they declared that both ancient trees would share the largest Sitka spruce title.

Story over, right?

Well, not exactly.

The Sitka Spruce dispute simmered until December 2006, when a fierce winter storm opened up an old "lightening scar" about 80 feet up the trunk of Oregon's landmark Sitka Spruce. The tree's days were numbered, but it was allowed to die a natural death. The end came just a year later when the 700-year-old tree broke in half during another unusually harsh winter storm. Fans of the first Oregon Heritage Tree were devastated, and some people even drove out to pay their last respects to the fallen giant. But rather than chop down the trunk and remove the fallen tree's sections, officials decided to let everything stay right where it landed so visitors can come by and watch the lifecycle of the forest in action.

The remains of Oregon's Sitka spruce, also known as the Klootchy Creek Giant and the Seaside Spruce, are located in Klootchy Creek Park, southeast of Seaside on US 26. Keep an eye out for the sign.

Fed by the Sea
Seaside

Founded in 1937, the small, family-owned Seaside Aquarium is one of the oldest aquariums on the West Coast. Once the abode of Clara the Seal, who'd let onlookers know she was hungry by putting her flippers in her mouth, today the aquarium is home to a well-respected breeding program for harbor seals.

But long before an army of seals, Dungeness crabs, sea anemones, wolf eels, and other sea creatures took up residence here, the building housed an indoor swimming pool, or natatorium, for people. Back in the 1920s cold seawater was pumped into the building via a pipe and then heated to a comfortable bath-like temperature for swimmers. Balconies allowed non-bathers to keep a watchful eye on friends and family members splashing about below.

The natatorium closed down in the early 1930s, but the pipe that brought sea water in for swimmers is still used to bring in water to fill the aquarium tanks. Down in the basement, where the deep end of the pool used to be, there are now three rock-filled holes. Piped-in sea-water is filtered through the rocks so that the water pumped into the aquarium tanks is clear enough to allow visitors to see sea creatures who now call the aquarium home. Depending on the tide, the intake end of the pipe can often be seen sticking up, somewhat eerily, on the beach.

The Seaside Aquarium is open year-round and is located on the beach at the end of Second Avenue and North Promenade, 2 blocks north of the Seaside Turnaround at 200 North Prom. For more information call (503) 738-6211 or go to www.seasideaquarium.com.

Say Cheese!
Tillamook

Ever since 1893, when Peter McIntosh brought his cheddar cheese recipe to town, Tillamook has been awash in curds and whey. Today the high-tech Tillamook Cheese Factory churns out a wide variety of cheese, ice cream, butter, sour cream, and yogurt products, but every block of award-winning cheddar is still made using McIntosh's original recipe.

Visitors are welcome at the factory, and each year more than a million folks take the self-guided tour to learn how milk from the area's 28,000 cows gets turned into all manner of dairy-dependent products. And while it's certainly fun (and educational) to learn how the vats of curds and whey are transformed into Swiss, cheddar, mozzarella, and Monterey Jack cheeses, by far the most popular part of the tour is the end. That's when the tiny cheese cubes are handed out as free samples. In fact, according to factory officials, in 2008 Tillamook Cheese guests sampled about 4,851,000 cubes, the equivalent of more than 15,000 pounds of cheese.

★ ★

If you go, don't fill up on the cheese cubes. The visitor center has a full-service restaurant, a fudge counter with more than twenty different year-round flavors, and an ice-cream counter serving close to forty varieties, including chocolate peanut butter, Oregon strawberry, and the ever-popular Udderly Chocolate.

The Tillamook Cheese Factory is located at 4175 US 101 North in Tillamook. For more information call (503) 815-1300 or visit www .tillamookcheese.com.

Got milk?
Tillamook County Creamery Association

Surprising Soup

While many recipes call for cheese, this cheesy vegetarian soup has a surprising ingredient: beer.

Beer Cheddar Soup

4 tablespoons Tillamook butter

4 tablespoons flour

3 cups milk

1 tablespoon garlic, minced

salt and pepper to taste

1 teaspoon crushed red chilies, chopped

2 cups Tillamook Extra Sharp Cheddar Cheese, shredded

¾ cup dark beer

Heat butter in sauté pan. Add flour and cook on low heat. Stir mixture until it starts to bubble. Do not allow to brown. Pull off fire and set aside. Heat milk in sauce pan until it is just ready to boil. Add garlic, salt and pepper, and crushed red chilies. Stir mixture until just before boiling. Add half of flour/butter mixture (roux) and stir with wire whisk until at a low simmer. Additional roux may be added to thicken. Stir constantly to avoid burning. Turn down heat and add Tillamook Extra Sharp Cheddar Cheese and beer. Stir to allow cheese to melt. Texture should be smooth to the touch. May be reheated on low temp. (Do not boil.)

Recipe by Billy Hahn, Executive Chef, Jake's Famous Crawfish Restaurant, Portland. Courtesy of Tillamook County Creamery Association.

✦ ✦

Mac 'n' Cheese
Tillamook

For many kids and probably an equal number of adults, macaroni and cheese is the very definition of comfort food. Thomas Jefferson supposedly served a version of this dish at the White House in 1802, and Kraft Foods currently sells more than a million boxes a year of the macaroni and cheese dinner it first introduced back in 1937.

The folks at the Tillamook County Creamery Association—makers of the award-winning Tillamook cheddar cheese—are all for a diet rich in macaroni and cheese. In fact, in 2005 the organization began sponsoring a Macaroni and Cheese Recipe Contest. Each year contestants in at least eight western cities are invited to submit unique homemade macaroni and cheese recipes that are then evaluated by chefs

Macaroni Lobster Casserole: An example of culinary creativity at its best.
Tillamook County Creamery Association

and celebrities for use of ingredients, taste, and creativity. Finalists are invited to attend local cook-offs and compete for prizes of cash, dining certificates at sponsoring restaurants, and up to twenty-five pounds of, you guessed it, Tillamook cheese. Regional winners get a free trip to the grand macaroni and cheese cook-off in Portland.

So far, winning recipes have featured lobster, truffle essence, shrimp, and artichoke hearts but the contest is still young—so don't be shy about submitting your own cheesy creation. For deadlines and entry rules, go to www.macaroniandcheeseandcheese.com/contest.

Don't Hog the Backseat

Tillamook

Forget sack races. Forget pie-eating contests. Each August the Tillamook County Fair packs 'em in with the Pig-N-Ford Races. As in live squirming, squealing pigs and real, classic Model T Fords.

It sounds like an unusual combination, but fair organizers trace the idea for the races back to 1925, when a pig being transported through town by a couple of local residents escaped. As the story goes, folks had so much fun watching the drivers try to catch the pig and get it back into their Model T that the escapade got turned into an event at the county fair.

Model Ts haven't been built since 1927, but in Tillamook there's a club whose members own ten working models that are used each year for the event. To win the race, a driver must complete three laps around a track and keep a different pig on board as their passenger for each lap.

Before starting out a driver must run to a pig pen, grab a pig, and hold onto it while hand-cranking the car. Then the driver and the pig must get in the car and take off down the track. If the pig escapes— and it usually does—the driver must chase it down and convince the little porker to get back in the car. When each lap is finished, the driver must stop the engine, put the pig back in the pen, grab another pig, and start over.

★ ★

Who wants a ride?
Josh Balmer

"We used to do it with seventy-pound pigs," says one regular con-
testant, "but now the fair organizers provide porkers that are thirty
pounds or less. Still, it helps if you're young and light on your feet
because most of the time the pigs aren't too happy to be getting
grabbed and thrown in the car. Some of them will bite you, pinch you,
poop on you, or scratch you with their hooves. Others seem happy as a
pig in, uh, mud to be going for the ride. You just never know."

The Pig-N-Ford Races are part of the annual Tillamook County Fair,
which is usually held during the first full week in August. To get there
take US 101 to Tillamook and turn onto Third Street. Stay in the
right-hand lane until you reach a V in the road and veer to the right.
Stay on this street (Third Street) for about 1.5 miles until you reach
the Tillamook County Fairgrounds. For more information contact the
fairgrounds at (503) 842-2272 or visit www.tillamookfair.com.

Record-Breaking Building

Tillamook

During WWII the U.S. Navy stationed a fleet of blimps along the east and west coasts. Each airship was 252 feet long and filled with 425,000 cubic feet of helium. These "K-class" blimps had a range of 2,000 miles and could stay in the air for three days at a time, so they were ideally suited for antisubmarine patrol and for escorting ship convoys out to sea. The blimps also trailed targets for fighter-plane practice.

To store off-duty dirigibles, the navy built seventeen seven-acre blimp hangars. They used the exact same blueprint for each building, and each clear-span wooden structure was fifteen stories high, more than 1,000 feet long, and built with fire-retardant lumber. Tillamook's dairy land was chosen as the site for two of those hangars in part because the countryside offered mild weather and the largest flat area on the Oregon and Washington coast. Tillamook was also protected to the west by three capes.

Unfortunately, Tillamook's Hangar A burned down in 1992. (Turns out the chemicals that make wood fire-retardant eventually leach out.) But Hangar B is still around, and it now shares the title of World's Largest Clear-Span Wooden Building with the six other still-intact blimp hangars around the country.

Hangar B is now also home to the Tillamook Air Museum, which houses a flight simulator, a collection of more than thirty WWII "war birds," and historical films and displays about the construction of the building and the blimps that were once based there. Tillamook's blimps were outfitted with bombs, depth charges, and guns, and did see some action during the war. Of course, says a museum curator, the navy did its best to maintain good relations with the dairy farmers in the community. Sometimes that required the utmost in diplomatic skills. For example, when a blimp was running low on helium, sandbags on board would often be thrown overboard to lighten the load. Once, when those sandbags landed on an unsuspecting cow in

★ ★

Trivia

Blimp Hangar Bio

Length: 1,072 feet

Height: 192 feet (more than fifteen stories)

Width: 296 feet

Area: More than seven acres (enough to play six football games)

Doors: 120 feet high; six sections each weighing thirty tons; 220-foot-wide opening. The sections roll on railroad tracks.

Catwalks: Two catwalks, each 137 feet above the hangar deck

a pasture, the navy was quick to offer reparations. That sandbagged cow suddenly gained great value as the farmer remembered that the sandbagged cow had been the biggest producer in the herd.

In addition to the vintage airplanes and historical displays, the Tillamook Air Museum hosts fly-ins, car shows, and other special events. The museum is located 2 miles south of Tillamook, just off US 101. Turn at the flashing light next to the A-4 aircraft displayed on a pole. For additional information call (503) 842-1130 or go to www .tillamookair.com.

2

Portland

Portland, Oregon's largest city, has plenty of nicknames. Known as the Rose City, due mostly to the presence of the International Rose Test Gardens at Washington Park, the city also answers to "Stumptown" (a logging reference), "Bridgetown" (eight bridges lead to and from downtown), "Puddletown" (yup, the

The Portland penny.
Oregon Historical Society Collection

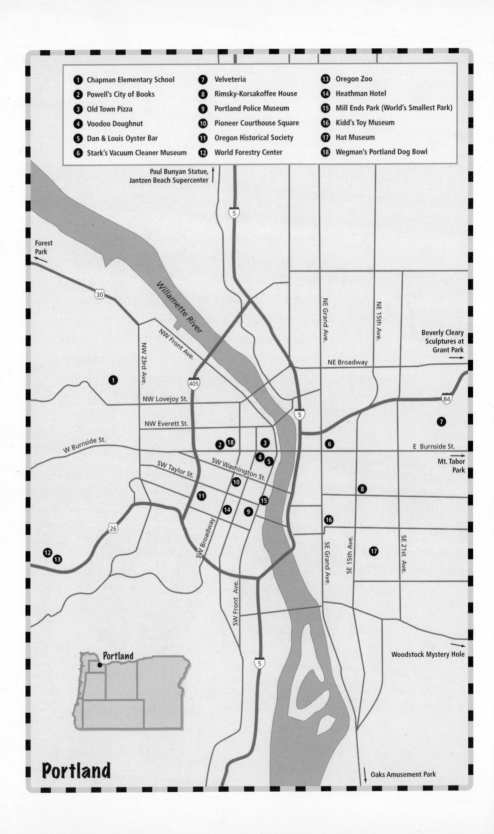

Portland

1. Chapman Elementary School
2. Powell's City of Books
3. Old Town Pizza
4. Voodoo Doughnut
5. Dan & Louis Oyster Bar
6. Stark's Vacuum Cleaner Museum
7. Velveteria
8. Rimsky-Korsakoffee House
9. Portland Police Museum
10. Pioneer Courthouse Square
11. Oregon Historical Society
12. World Forestry Center
13. Oregon Zoo
14. Heathman Hotel
15. Mill Ends Park (World's Smallest Park)
16. Kidd's Toy Museum
17. Hat Museum
18. Wegman's Portland Dog Bowl

Paul Bunyan Statue,
Jantzen Beach Supercenter

Forest Park

Willamette River

Beverly Cleary Sculptures at Grant Park

NW Front Ave.

NW 23rd Ave.

NE Grand Ave.

NE 15th Ave.

NE Broadway

NW Lovejoy St.

NW Everett St.

W Burnside St.

E Burnside St.

Mt. Tabor Park

SW Taylor St.

SW Washington St.

SW Broadway

SW Front Ave.

SE Grand Ave.

SE 15th Ave.

SE 21st Ave.

Woodstock Mystery Hole

Oaks Amusement Park

rain), and several other monikers, including "Rivercity." But when the city was first being named, there was a 50-50 chance it would have been officially dubbed Boston.

In 1843 Asa Lovejoy loaned William Overton 25 cents so he could file a land claim on 640 acres along the Willamette River. In return Lovejoy got half the land. Two years later, however, a still-cash-poor Overton sold his half of the land claim to Francis Pettygrove. The two new business partners agreed it was time to name their town, but disagreed about what to name it. Lovejoy wanted to name it for his hometown, Boston, Massachusetts. Pettygrove hoped to honor his hometown, Portland, Maine. They agreed to flip a coin, and Pettygrove from Portland won the wager—best two out of three.

The Oregon Historical Society (at 1200 Southwest Park Avenue) displays the copper coin used in "the flip." and that's a great place to start exploring the city. But don't stop there: Curiosities in the Rose City include the world's largest independent bookstore, a museum of velvet paintings, and the "World's Smallest Park."

Not Your Kid's Soap Box Derby

In 1912, just three years after the 195 acres around Mount Tabor were set aside as an in-city park for Portlanders, city officials discovered volcanic cinders on-site and announced that the mountain was actually a dormant volcano. No one got too excited; in fact, the cinders came in handy as paving material for the park roads. Today Portland is proud to be one of only two cities in the continental United States with extinct volcanoes within the city limits. (The other one is Bend, Oregon.)

When the weather is clear, Mount Tabor offers great views of Mount Hood, downtown Portland, and the West Hills, and it's a popular year-round destination for low-key activities such as jogging and tennis. But once each year, in late August or early September, all hell breaks loose when the park's winding, cinder-paved roads are transformed into a racetrack and dozens of costumed men and women

★ ★

A few final touches might be in order before climbing up on your soap box.
Don Daugherty, Tranquil Velocity

climb into strange-looking, nonmotorized vehicles and willingly hurtle themselves down a mile-long course as part of the Portland Adult Soap Box Derby. The gravity-driven "cars" can be made of anything, including metal, wood, and milk cartons. The materials just can't cost more than $300.

This is clearly not your son's or daughter's soap box derby. For starters, there are the rules, which, among other things, mandate that cars must have "functional brakes (no Fred Flintstone brakes)" and weigh under 500 pounds. That weight limit is a new rule: According to the derby Web site, the 500-pound rule was put into place "to prevent road rash, broken arms, destroyed knees and generally horrible injuries caused by being dragged along the pavement under a 1,000 pound car."

Yikes!

★ ★

This is the sort of event where rules also address weaponry: "Liquid water is the only acceptable weapon or projectile which may be deployed from or against any car (water balloons are acceptable)." And, "No pyrotechnics, fire, or fireworks are allowed as part of any car."

That still leaves plenty of room for creativity and fun—and prizes. Past races have featured cars shaped like everything from dung beetles to pirate ships, and contestants have shown up wearing everything from helmets topped by disco balls to practically nothing at all. And folks who don't win a trophy for Best Costume or Best Engineering can still go home with the Lame Duck Award, which is presented to the car and driver whose trip down the track ends up taking the longest.

Mount Tabor Park is located at Southeast Sixtieth Avenue and Salmon Street in Portland. For more information about the park call Portland Parks and Recreation at (503) 823-2223 or visit www.portlandonline.com/parks. For more information about the Portland Adult Soap Box Derby, go to www.soapboxracer.com.

Hold Tight to Your Food

It looks just like an old house down a sort of dark street in a kind of weird place. There's no sign out front, but for more than a quarter century those in the know with a yen for coffee, decadent desserts, live classical music, and a bit of unpredictable zaniness have found their way here—again and again.

The slightly off-kilter name should tip you off: It's called the Rimsky-Korsakoffee House, a blended homage to nineteenth-century Russian classical music composer Nicolai Rimsky-Korsakov and the Northwest's official beverage. That explains the live classical music and, of course, the coffee drinks. But there's really no explaining the tables and the decorations, which can be surprising, alarming, and quite curious.

As owner Goody Cable explains it, each cloth-and-glass-topped table is named for a different classical composer and has a "pseudo elegant" decor, with delicate flowers and soft candlelight. Everything

★ ★

A previous customer?
Jacquie Jones

looks quite normal. But once you're seated, beware. Several tables are not at all what they seem.

One table elevates 18 inches every forty-five minutes "and just keeps going," says Cable. "And when it reaches its full height, it begins a very slow descent." Another table rotates very slowly, so diners not paying attention can look up to find their dessert in front of their dining partner. Then there's the Rachmaninoff table: Staff members can send this table shaking by pushing a button installed in the kitchen. "And," admits Cable, "there's my favorite: the Steven Sondheim table. It disappears altogether through a slit in a wall."

Reviewers consistently give the desserts high marks. But it's the unisex bathroom with the underwater theme—and a few surprises—that regularly induces screams.

The Rimsky-Korsakoffee House is located in a restored Victorian home at 708 Southeast Twelfth Avenue, near Alder Street in Portland. There's no sign out front; just look for the folks lined up on the sidewalk. For more information call (503) 232-2640.

Tubs, Teeth, and Tours

Carye Bye is a consummate cataloger and, at times, the crafty coordinator of some of Portland's most curious places and events. Several times a year, she organizes wacky in-city bike rides, such as the Bunny on a Bike Ride and the Pretty Dress Ride. She's also the curator of the Bathtub Art Museum, a collection of more than 300 vintage, handmade, one-of-a-kind, and modern-day bathtub-themed postcards displayed in a series of on-line galleries. Cards in the "Beauty and the Bath" and the "Peeping Tom" galleries, for example, are filled with offbeat and, at times, somewhat risqué images, but nothing that couldn't have gone through the U.S. mail.

Bye digs her teeth into Portland's offbeat places.
Illustration by Carye Bye

★ ★

Once in a while, Bye's enthusiasm for bathtubs bubbles over and she takes some of her postcard collection off-line to exhibit at venues around Portland. Exhibitions have been held at a library, a cafe, a barbershop, a video rental store, and, appropriately enough, a plumbing supply store.

Bye's interests go way beyond bathtubs and bikes, though. She's a connoisseur of Portland's curious, small museums and creates artwork to commemorate her favorites, such as the Museum of Dental Anomalies at the Oregon Health & Sciences University Dental School.

You can find the Bathtub Art Museum at www.bathtubmuseum .org. To find out about Bye's other favorite small museums in Portland, see http://hiddenportland.com.

Drink Up Downtown

Remember that saying "Water, water everywhere, but not a drop to drink"?

Not in Portland. Throughout the city you'll see fountains flowing with free drinking water, courtesy of the Portland Water Bureau.

The tradition dates back to 1896, when the Portland Water Committee began providing free water for the city's public drinking fountains as a symbol of hospitality and abundance. In 1912 lumberman and civic leader Simon Benson went with the flow and donated $10,000 for the creation of twenty elegant four-bowl bronze drinking fountains for the downtown area. Teetotaler Benson hoped that the fountains, which became known as Benson Bubblers, would encourage his workers and others to drink pure water instead of the liquor that flowed at local saloons.

Did it work? It's hard to tell: While Benson claimed that business at downtown bars dropped by up to 40 percent after the fountains were installed, no official surveys were made. Today there are plenty of bars and more than fifty Benson-style Bubblers in downtown Portland. And between 5 a.m. and 10 p.m. daily, each four-bowled bubbler offers a free, refreshing drink for up to four thirsty folks at a time.

No waiting at the Benson Bubblers.

Free drinking fountains are great, but Portland has dozens of intriguing and unusual decorative municipal fountains as well. For example, the bronze Skidmore Fountain (at Southwest First Avenue and Ankeny Street) sits at what was once the center of Portland. The fountain—designed to provide drinking water for people, horses, and dogs—is Portland's oldest piece of public art. It was built in 1888 using the $5,000 seed money left for just that purpose by Stephen Skidmore, a businessman and druggist who had arrived in Portland by covered wagon. The neoclassical fountain features two maidens supporting a bronze basin and is a popular gathering spot for visitors to Portland's Saturday Market. And although the water flowing here and in other decorative fountains about town is now chlorinated and not fit for drinking, freshwater is still piped into the low-level troughs for city police horses.

If you keep your eyes peeled, you'll notice plenty of other unusual fountains around town. Near Pioneer Courthouse Square and along downtown Max Light Rail tracks, look for Animals in Pools, a series of ten fountains offering cavorting opportunities for twenty-five bears, otters, and other bronze animals on Yamhill and Morrison Streets, between Southwest Fifth and Sixth Avenues. The Elk Fountain, on Southwest Main Street, between Third and Fourth Avenues and the Plaza Blocks, was a gift from David P. Thompson, who drove sheep to Portland over the Oregon Trail and who served as Portland's mayor from 1879 to 1882.

For more information about these and other city fountains, including one dubbed the Bathtub Fountain, go to www.portlandonline .com/water and enter "fountains" in the search box for a download-able self-guided tour brochure."

Bubbler for Bowser

The Benson Bubblers placed around town by philanthropist Simon Benson have been quenching thirsts since 1912. Over the years these drinking fountains have also served up artistic inspiration.

In February 2002, for example, a fountain named Portland Dog Bowl was unveiled in the city's North Park Blocks. Commissioned by the now-defunct Pearl Arts Foundation for $176,000, the sculpture was designed by noted Weimaraner dog photographer William Wegman. He described it as his homage to the city's Benson Bubblers and as an in-city amenity for dogs—though when it's filled with water, birds, cats, horses, and occasional people have made use of it.

Set into the grass in the North Park Blocks across from the Custom

A place where art meets life.
Ross Reynolds

House between Northwest Everett and Northwest Davis streets, Wegman's Portland Dog Bowl fountain can be somewhat easy to miss. That is, if you're a person. Dogs seem to have no trouble finding the ground-level sculpture that measures 8 by 10 feet and is composed of checkerboard granite tiles and a cast-iron dog bowl pushed off to one side—as if a thirsty pup has just passed by.

Hole of Mystery

There are black holes in space, hypothetical wormholes in physics, and car-gobbling sinkholes that are found, for some reason, most often in the South. In a Portland neighborhood, there's something possibly more puzzling: the Woodstock Mystery Hole.

"No one would have suspected from looking at an ordinary wild blackberry patch in a suburban backyard that Oregon's most incredible archeological site lies waiting beneath," explains Mr. E. Mann, the hole's discoverer and caretaker.

★ ★

What's certain is that there is a hole. What's uncertain is just about everything else about the hole. But those who have been lucky enough—and brave enough—to venture inside the hole, and who are willing and able to use their "natural psychic abilities," are promised a rare peek at a "Giant Double Arch," a stupendous "Gaping Tunnel," cryptic rock inscriptions, and many other natural, or maybe unnatural, oddities.

How was the Mystery Hole dug in the first place? The hole's owner doesn't know. Or isn't saying. "The absence of pick and shovel marks points to crude methods by a primitive people. However, this is given by some researchers as evidence of extraterrestrial activity. Indeed, marks not unlike laser-blasting are clearly visible on the walls of this gaping cavern, adding fuel to the fires of debate. Most experts and theorists do agree on one thing—it was not created by natural forces."

OK, never mind. But how deep is it?

Again, Mr. E. Mann doesn't know. Or won't say much more than "it goes all the way to the bottom" and is "very deep."

What happens if you go down into the hole and breathe the "Enchanting Vapors of Encouragement"? No one knows for sure, but legend has it that the "vapors" can cure illness and bring love "in less than a month" and "more money than you know what to do with." Or perhaps not.

Sound mysterious? That's why they call it the Woodstock Mystery Hole.

Unfortunately, Mystery Hole tours have been, mysteriously, suspended. But even when they were offered, many visitors may have turned back when asked to sign a liability waiver certifying: ". . . I must be out of my mind to climb down into a damp, dark hole when I'm perfectly safe where I am."

Still curious? Virtual tours can be enjoyed on the Woodstock Mystery Hole Web site: www.barronmind.com.

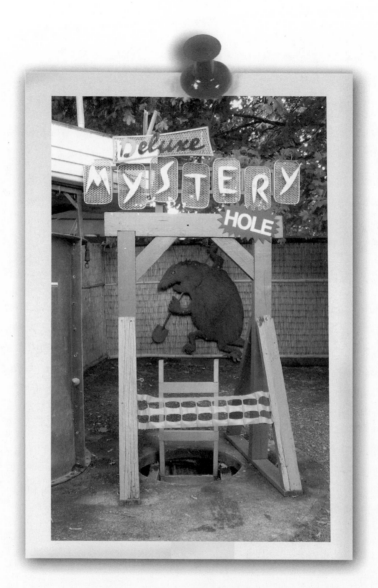

Maybe the mole dug the hole.
Barron

Past Portlanders

Many famous folks have had strong associations with Portland. Here are just a few:

Mel Blanc—The voice of Bugs Bunny, Elmer Fudd, Woody Woodpecker, and countless other cartoon classics grew up in Portland.

Clark Gable—Before this big-eared heartthrob made it big in Hollywood, Gable spent time in Oregon, first in Astoria and then in Portland, working as a salesman, as an actor, and in lumberyards. In Portland he met and eventually married Josephine Dillon, an actress more than ten years his senior, who helped Gable move up in the world by teaching him etiquette and convincing him to fix his teeth.

Matt Groening—the creator of *The Simpsons*, *Futurama*, and *Life in Hell* grew up in Portland. References to Portland people and places show up in his work. In *The Simpsons*, Flanders Street was the inspiration for the name of Ned Flanders, the Simpsons' irritating next-door neighbor. Reverend Lovejoy, the show's minister, gets his name from Lovejoy Street. Groening doesn't just take from the city: Legend has it that it was the cartoonist himself, a 1972 graduate of Lincoln High School, who drew a picture of Homer Simpson in a wet slab of cement outside the school on the east side of Southwest Eighteenth Avenue, south of Salmon Street. No one else has claimed credit for that artwork, not even Bart Simpson. All he's said is: "I didn't do it, nobody saw me do it, there's no way you can prove anything!"

★ ★

Ride Rare Carousels

While there were once more than 10,000 carousels around the country, today fewer than 200 of those classic originals are still operating. Oregon has two of them.

The Jantzen Beach shopping center is home to a seventy-two-horse carousel designed and built in 1921 by the C. W. Parker Amusement Company. It's a large, four-abreast model with elaborate horses and many one-of-a-kind animals. The carousel operates during regular mall hours and costs just $2 per ride. Jantzen Beach Super-Center is just north of Portland, adjacent to the Interstate Bridge on the Washington border. Take exit 308 off I-5. For more information call (503) 286-9103 or go to www.jantzenbeachsupercenter.com.

Put down your packages and hop on a rare carousel at Jantzen Beach Center
Jantzen Beach Center

★ ★

Oaks Amusement Park, near the Sellwood Bridge in Portland, is one of the country's oldest amusement parks. It has a 1920 Herschell-Spillman Noah's Ark, or menagerie, carousel that operates during park hours, which vary by season. For details call (503) 233-5777 or visit www.oakspark.com.

Too Many Toys

Frank Kidd (yes, that's his real name) grew up helping out with his family's car parts business. For a while he collected full-size antique cars, but says he later realized that toy cars took up less room—and were lots more fun to play with.

At first Kidd kept his collection at home, but as it grew he needed more space. He originally put his toy cars and antique mechanical

Antique toys on parade.

No bones about it, this bank welcomes your money.

banks on spare shelves at his Portland auto parts store. But he soon ran out of space there and so spread out into a storefront nearby. For a while the collection was a word-of-mouth treasure passed along by truck drivers, salespeople, and do-it-yourselfers hunting for auto parts who stumbled into the store. But word got out, and today Kidd's 10,000-piece collection of toys from the early 1900s through the 1980s fills an entire building and is open to the public as a museum.

Given Kidd's background, it is no surprise that the collection features lots of little vehicles: passenger cars, delivery trucks, fire trucks, and several hundred toy motorcycles. But there are also dolls dressed in gas station uniforms, character toys, police badges from Oregon and Washington, toy ray guns and cap guns, lots of railroad memorabilia, and much more.

★ ★

Kidd's collection of antique banks is especially impressive. Some are extremely detailed but no bigger than a golf ball. Others are shaped like everything from frogs and dogs to Santa Claus and a black, red, and yellow Ferris wheel. Some are dainty but do the job. For example, a mechanical cast-iron favorite features a girl who skips rope whenever a penny is deposited.

No need to deposit a penny or anything else when you visit Kidd's Toy Museum, though, because admission is free. Find it at 1301 Southeast Grand Avenue. For information about hours and directions, call (503) 233-7807 or visit http://kiddstoymuseum.com/Index.html.

Rolling Amusements

Opened in 1905, just days before the Lewis and Clark Exposition, Oaks Park is among the oldest amusement parks in the country (some

Fun and games ahead at Oaks Amusement Park.
Illustration by Carye Bye

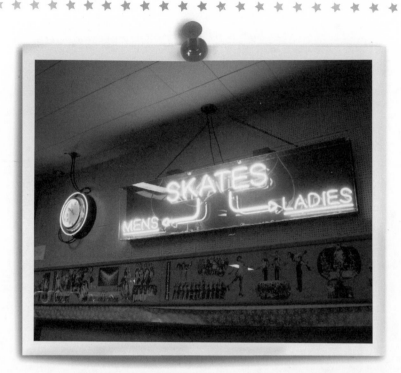

Take a spin at the oldest continuously operated skating rink.
Ross Reynolds

say the oldest) and, over the years, it's definitely been home to a wide variety of curiosities.

In the early days Portlanders who made their way to the park were rewarded with entertaining treats that ranged from band concerts led by John Philip Sousa to outdoor movies, high divers, flagpole sitters, trapeze acts, and a menagerie of animals that included monkeys, bears, lions, a roller-skating elephant, and a family of ostriches. "One day, an ostrich leaned over and ate a diamond stick pin off a man's lapel," a park staff member says, "and someone had to be hired to sit with that ostrich and wait for the pin to, uh, pass."

The ostriches, lions, and monkeys are long gone, but some animals are still here. The park's rare circa 1920 Herschell-Spillman Noah's Ark carousel with two rows of hand-carved jumping animals is on the National Register of Historic Places.

★ ★

Equally historic is the park's skating rink, which opened in 1905 and is now the oldest continuously operating skating rink in the country. In its early days a brass band played live music from a loft directly above the rink. Later a series of increasingly larger—and louder—Wurlitzer organs replaced the band above the rink. Today Oaks Park is the only rink offering skaters live Wurlitzer music.

That the skating rink still exists is also somewhat of a marvel. In 1948 a flood put the entire park underwater for a month. Rides were warped, and the 100-by-200-foot wooden floor of the skating rink took five months to repair. To keep the floor from warping in another flood, engineers tried "floating" the floor on a system of more than fifty-five airtight barrels. The design worked: During two subsequent floods (in 1964 and 1996) rink employees armed with chain saws cut the floatable floor from the rest of the building and, when floodwaters receded, the floor was fine.

Oaks Amusement Park is located on the eastern edge of the Willamette River in Portland, just below the Sellwood Bridge at 1 Southeast Spokane Street. The park is open weekends only in the spring and early fall and daily throughout the summer. The skating rink operates year-round. For directions and hours call (503) 233-5777 or visit www.oakspark.com.

Uninvited Guest

With opulent Italian Renaissance details, a eucalyptus-paneled Tea Court, and the best amenities and appointments possible, the Heathman Hotel was heralded for being "as modern as human ingenuity and talent could possibly make it" when it opened in 1927. Years of wear and tear took its toll on the grand dame, but after a $16 million restoration in the 1980s, the hotel received National Historic Landmark status.

The costly renovation hasn't done anything, however, to deter the ghost that reportedly haunts rooms whose numbers end in 03. Time after time the front desk receives phone calls from guests who have

One for the Books

A less spooky link to the Heathman's past guests is a collection of more several thousand signed first-edition books by authors who have stayed at the historic downtown hotel. There are cookbooks and history books, fiction, nonfiction, and science fiction by a veritable who's who of writers, including Tom Wolfe, Wallace Stegner, David Sedaris, David McCullough, John Updike, Ken Kesey, Julia Child, William Stafford, Joyce Carol Oates, five Nobel Peace Prize winners, four U.S. Poet Laureates, at least twenty-five Pulitzer Prize winners, and many others. New additions are added on a regular basis, because the Heathman is a popular place for authors on book tours to stay when in town.

The hotel doesn't have enough room to display the entire collection, and some of the rarer editions are kept under lock and key. However, at any one time at least 800 signed books are displayed on locked shelves in the cozy Authors Library on the hotel's mezzanine

A treasure trove of signed first editions.
John Rizzo

level. Hotel guests are welcome to curl up in a chair with a book signed by a favorite author or check out a book to read during their stay. And everyone is welcome to stop by during the open library tours held each Thursday evening from 5:30 to 7:00 p.m.

★ ★

checked into their freshly cleaned rooms, gone out for a stroll, and returned to find that a towel has been used, a glass of water has been left on a desk, or chairs in the room have been rearranged. But a check of the electronic key record shows that no one has entered the room.

A psychic staying in Room 803 claims to have seen a ghost at the foot of her bed and theorized that since the strange occurrences were reported from the column of rooms between 303 and 1003, that perhaps someone who jumped to his or her death from the hotel roof now returns to haunt the rooms he or she passed on the way down.

The Heathman Hotel is located in downtown Portland, at 1001 Southwest Broadway at Salmon Street. For more information call (503) 241-4100 or visit www.heathmanhotel.com.

Big Guy on Duty

Known best as the oversize, oxen-assisted folk hero of the upper Midwest, mythical lumberjack Paul Bunyan is commemorated with giant statues throughout the country. Travelers will encounter big Bunyans in Maine, Minnesota, Michigan, California, and plenty of places in between, including Portland, Oregon.

The Rose City's 37-foot-tall, six-ton likeness of Paul Bunyan was created in 1959 to honor Oregon's timber industry and to commemorate the Oregon Centennial Exposition, which was held in the livestock yards near the Kenton neighborhood just north of downtown. Designed by the owner of Kenton Machine Works, Portland's Paul Bunyan was a community project that drew on the skills of local welders, ironworkers, and plasterers. Those hard-working fellows gave Bunyan a traditional red and white plaid lumberjack shirt, a huge pair of black boots, a giant ax, a full black beard, and a set of pearly white teeth.

During the centennial fair the statue served as a welcome sign for travelers crossing the Columbia River from Washington into Oregon. After the fair, the statue marked the site of a tourist information

Don't ever give this man a chain saw.
Ross Reynolds

★ ★

booth. That lasted until about 1964, when the opening of I-5 rerouted visitors away from the neighborhood.

For years Kenton was better known for its crime statistics than for being the home of the giant statue. But now that the area is getting gentrified, Bunyan is getting some tender loving care and attention. The local transit agency, Tri-Met, moved the statue 50 feet, to a small plaza, to make room for the light-rail line. The big guy got repainted and refreshed. And in early 2009 Portland's lumberjack statue was given his own spot on the National Register of Historic Places.

Portland's Paul Bunyan statue is located at the intersection of North Denver and North Interstate Avenue in the North Portland neighborhood of Kenton.

Hanging 'round the Square

Spend even a bit of time in Portland and it's a good bet you'll end up at Pioneer Courthouse Square in the heart of downtown at 715 South-west Morrison. The open-air piazza is sometimes referred to as the city's "living room" and, rain or shine, it serves as a year-round trans-portation node, meeting spot, event venue, and place to hang around.

The scene is sweetened by a variety of unusual historic and artistic elements, including bronze chessboards, Roman columns, and a mile post sign showing the distances to far-off locations such as Portland, Maine, and Tipperary. Curiously, the other Portland is listed as being 2,540 miles away, while it's actually more than 3,000 miles. Tipperary, on the other hand, is correctly tagged as being "a long way" away.

If you can, be on hand at noon when the square's weather machine comes to life for just two minutes. There's a fanfare of whis-tles, mist, lights, and sound. And, depending on the weather, one of three symbols appears: a dragon for stormy days of rain and winds; a blue heron for days of drizzle, mist, or transitional weather; or the rarer-seen stylized sun, promising a clear, sunny day.

While in the square be sure to look down at the 68,000-plus named bricks. Sold to raise money to build and maintain the square, most of the bricks bear the names of local citizens and businesses. But look carefully and you'll find bricks bearing some very familiar names, including Elvis, Jimi Hendrix, John Lennon, Dan Rather, Sherlock Holmes, Frodo Baggins, God, and George Washington. As a courtesy, there's even an online "Celebrity Brick Map" at www .pioneercourthousesquare.org/PCS_CelebrityBrickMap.pdf.

Cloudy today with rain developing this evening.
Ross Reynolds

★ ★

Soul of the City

The first person to own the Pioneer Courthouse Square property was Elijah Hill. In 1849 the shoemaker purchased the land for twenty-four dollars—and a pair of boots. The site was later home to Portland's first public school, a hotel, and eventually a parking lot. The city got hold of the land in 1974 and officially dedicated Pioneer Courthouse Square for public use in 1984, on April 6, the city's birthday.

Between the Covers

Portland science-fiction and fantasy writer Ursula LeGuin called it "the mother monster of bookstores." The *Washington Post* called it a "bibliophile motherlode." As much tourist attraction as bookshop, Powell's City of Books may be the reason why Portlanders buy more books per capita than readers in any other city in the country. Or it may be the other way around.

Sprawling through three floors and an entire city block, Powell's is the largest independent brick-and-mortar bookstore in the country. (There are seven other Powell's stores scattered around the city, including several branches at the airport.) In the downtown store alone, there are more than a million new and used books, and just getting around the nine huge color-coded rooms requires a map, which the store happily hands out to the tune of more than 100,000 a year.

In addition to hundreds of author readings and book signings, Powell's offers in-store walking tours and has hosted at least two weddings. The store also has an art gallery and a coffee shop and is home to the West's only three-door elevator, which was specially

A GPS might be helpful.

designed to provide access to the building's half-stories.

Many customers have a special place in their heart for Powell's City of Books. Perhaps none more than the anonymous book lover whose ashes were mixed into the cement used to create the Pillar of Books at the store's northwest entrance at Southwest Eleventh Avenue and Northwest Couch Street. Composed of eight stone-versions of the world's great books, the 9-foot column includes Hamlet, War and Peace, The Odyssey, and the motto (in Latin and English) "Buy the Book, Read the Book, Enjoy the Book, Sell the Book."

Powell's City of Books is located at 1005 West Burnside Street in downtown Portland. For more information call (503) 228-0540 or visit www.powells.com.

Official Portland

Though it's known worldwide as "The City of Roses," the Portland City Council has curiously never passed a resolution making this the official city nickname. Nor has the rose ever been named Portland's official flower.

However, over the years the Portland City Council has taken the time to pass resolutions establishing a city song, a city flag, a city seal, a city bird (great blue heron) and a city slogan ("The City that Works").

For the Birds

It never ends as badly as Alfred Hitchcock's 1963 movie, *The Birds*, but unless you're prepared for it, the sudden appearance of up to 15,000 to 40,000 dark, noisy birds in the sky overhead can be quite unnerving.

For more than fifteen years now, thousands of migrating Vaux's swifts have made the tall chimney at Portland's Chapman Elementary School a stopover on their annual trip from Alaska and Canada to Mexico and South America. It's the largest known communal swift roost in the world and, like the return of students for fall classes, it happens like clockwork early each September.

The tiny 4-to-5-inch birds (referred to by some as "cigars with wings") would rather roost in big, hollow old-growth trees, but there aren't enough of those left in the woods anymore. So the rough surfaces and cracked bricks lining the school's chimney have become an urban alternative.

When the birds first appeared, back in the fall of 1994, the schoolchildren adopted the swifts as their mascot. When the weather turned chilly, teachers and students even volunteered to wear their

If you're a Vaux's swift, nothing says home like a chimney.
VernonDiPietroPhotographer.com

★ ★

coats and sweaters in class so that the school didn't have to turn on the furnace and risk roasting the roosting birds. Happily, gas heat now warms the school, and the chimney is set aside just for the birds.

These days the annual swift invasion is a community-wide celebration. Crowds of spectators show up each evening with blankets, picnics, cameras, and binoculars to witness clouds of birds massing and circling the chimney before dropping down into it to settle in for the night.

Chapman Elementary School is at 1445 Northwest Twenty-sixth Avenue and Northwest Pettygrove Street in Portland. The swifts usually arrive in late August or early September and stick around for a few weeks, entering the chimney each night around sunset. The Audubon Society of Portland organizes an annual Swift Watch. For more information call (503) 292-6855 or go to www.audubonportland.org.

These Things Really Suck

They suck—and that's why they're here.

Since 1932 the folks at Stark's Vacuums have been helping Portlanders find the perfect suction-production cleaning devices. Along the way this family-owned business has also acquired hundreds of vintage vacuum cleaners. Most have made their way here through trade-ins and donations, and some have been brought in by people who just couldn't bear to throw away grandma's old fifty-pound Eureka or Electrolux model.

No need to shed a tear. Stark's has set aside the carpeted back corner of their flagship store for the Vacuum Cleaner Museum, a collection of more than 300 vacuums that reaches back to the early and very inefficient hand-pumped contraptions from the late 1800s that were shaped like pogo sticks or ice-cream cones.

Wander through the museum and you'll see that dust-sucking really picked up after 1908, when someone figured out how to attach electric motors to the mechanical models. After that vacuums got everything from clutches and headlights to quick-release dirt traps. They also got sleek-sounding names, such as Silent Air,

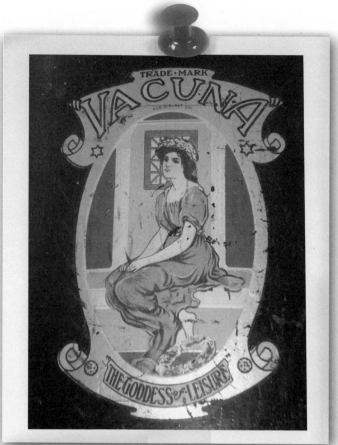

Who knew there was a goddess of vacuums?
Ross Reynolds

Cadillac, and Cinderella. One was even branded with the celestial image of Vacuna, the Goddess of Leisure.

Some vacuums here have surprising special features. One model doubles as a hair dryer and has attachments that serve as a neck vibrator, a clothes dryer, and a de-moth-er. Another multipurpose model conceals a heavy-duty vacuum inside a footstool, for those quick clean-ups in the den.

In addition to all the really old vacuums on display, there are

★ ★

vintage carpet sweepers, hand cleaners, and electric floor polishers. One of the newer models in the museum dates to the 1960s: The Halley's Comet Vacuum arrived from the factory spray-painted gold, bearing a special message under the lid for the modern homemaker. It reads: "The age of space, rocket race, push button leisure day. Be first to clean your jet-set home the Halley's Comet way."

Stark's Vacuum Cleaner Museum is located inside Stark's Vacuums at 107 Northeast Grand Avenue. For more information call (503) 232-4101 or visit www.starks.com.

Time to Eat the Doughnuts

If you consider doughnuts simply a Sunday morning treat or part of breakfast on the run, think again. The folks at Voodoo Doughnut keep the doors open twenty-four hours a day (twenty-one hours a day at their Voodoo Doughnut Too location) and no matter what time you arrive, it's a good bet that some sort of wacky doughnut-inspired activities will be taking place.

First, there's the menu, which can and does change often. Highlights include vegan doughnuts, a chocolate-glazed chocolate doughnut covered with cocoa puffs, a doughnut in the shape of a voodoo doll, an apple fritter as big as your head and, for a while there, doughnuts made with Nyquil glazing and Pepto-Bismol. Unfortunately (or fortunately), the Food and Drug Administration declared the drugstore-inspired doughnut to be an unhealthy cross between food and medicine and prohibited it from being sold side-by-side with sugar-laden pastries.

The doughnuts at Voodoo Doughnut are just part of the draw. There's also a full range of entertaining in-store events, including doughnut-eating contests on the first Friday of each month, live music and performances that lean to the bizarre, and the occasional commitment ceremony or legal wedding, complete with doughnuts and coffee, held under the Cruller Chandelier of Life and officiated by the licensed in-house ministers, Kenneth "Cat Daddy" Pogson and

Bet you can't even eat one.

Tres Shannon, who also happen to own the business.

And then there's the standing doughnut-eating challenge: If you can eat one of the giant "Tex-Ass" doughnuts—a giant glazed doughnut equal to four full-size doughnuts—in less than one minute and a half, or faster than the last record-breaker, your giant doughnut is free. Look for Voodoo Doughnut at 22 Southwest Third Avenue in Portland's Old Town neighborhood and Voodoo Doughnut Too at 1501 Northeast Davis. (They also deliver!) For more information, or to schedule a wedding or a commitment ceremony, call (503) 241-4704; the Web site is www.voodoodoughnut.com.

★ ★

Talented Troubadour

In 1941, long before he was a folk music legend, Woody Guthrie
was a twenty-eight-year-old struggling songwriter and singer in need
of a job. So when the Bonneville Power Authority offered Guthrie a
month-long assignment (pay: $266.66) writing songs, he packed up
his family and moved from California to Portland.

As "information consultant," Guthrie's job was to write songs for
the soundtrack of a documentary being produced to promote the
agency's hydroelectric projects, most notably the Grand Coulee Dam,
which stretches across the Columbia River in Washington State and
is North America's largest concrete structure. From his Portland base,
Guthrie rushed about the region, getting a feel for the Columbia
River area, the giant dam, and the impact the project was having on
the people who lived in the area's logging camps, farms, and rural
communities.

Guthrie ended up writing twenty-six songs during his thirty-day
assignment, including "Roll on Columbia, Roll On"; "Grand Coulee
Dam"; "Hard Travelin'"; and "Pastures of Plenty." Before leaving
Portland in June 1941, Guthrie recorded an acetate disc with eleven
of the songs. Only a few made it into the soundtrack of the documentary, which fell victim to budget troubles and wasn't completed
until 1948. Few people saw the film anyway: In 1953 all copies of
the documentary were destroyed after government officials learned
of Guthrie's leftist political leanings. The acetate disc and the song
sheets survived, however, and many of the tunes have become folk
standards. And in 1987 "Roll on Columbia, Roll On" was made the
official folk song of Washington State.

Talkative Timber

For more than thirty years, one of the most loved attractions at the
World Forestry Center's museum was a corny but cuddly 70-foot-tall
"talking" tree. Sadly, the sappy spokestree was retired as part of a

Armed but not dangerous.
World Forestry Center

major 2006 facility overhaul, but imagine the tales this fast-growing willow might tell if we could just get it to say a few words.

Instead we can only imagine who it was that went into the woods and left a perfectly good .22 caliber rifle leaning up against the crotch of this tree. And why they never came back for it. And why the rifle stayed put long enough for the tree to completely enclose the gun.

Today only a few inches of the barrel and the butt of the gun remain exposed on either side of the tree. Serving as a good

★ ★

reminder, perhaps, as to why it's important to keep moving.

Museum staff members have dubbed this curiosity the "armed willow" and display it among a forest of modern-day interactive exhibits that include a 60-foot forest canopy ride, a virtual smoke jumper exhibit, and a simulated river raft adventure ride.

The World Forestry Center Discovery Museum is located just outside downtown Portland, in Washington Park at 4033 Southwest Canyon Road. From US 26, take exit 72. For more information call (503) 228-1367 or visit www.worldforestrycenter.org.

Platter Chatter

The nautical-themed Dan & Louis Oyster Bar is as well known for its exotic decor as it is for a menu that includes a long list of seafood favorites, including oyster stew and oyster cocktails, which were the only items on the menu when Louis Wachsmuth opened the restaurant in 1907.

Wachsmuth's descendants have operated the sprawling restaurant for five generations now. And many of the items the founder first hung on the walls are still here, including beer steins, more than thirty ship models, all manner of maritime memorabilia, bits of flotsam and jetsam from Portland's history, and a collection of more than 200 antique plates, including what is certainly one of the world's largest accumulations of plates designed to serve oysters.

Of course, wherever there are oysters and oyster stew there are sure to be oyster crackers. Usually these are small crackers packaged in little plastic bags, but hanging in a place of honor in the entranceway of the restaurant is a plaque adorned with the World's Largest Oyster Cracker. It's more than a foot wide and, like any cracker that's been sitting around a while, it's a bit cracked. But it's definitely the same giant oyster cracker that was presented to the restaurant back in 1982 in recognition of the fact that the eatery had, to that date, served more than three million oyster crackers to its customers.

Dan & Louis Oyster Bar is located in downtown Portland at 208 Southwest Ankeny Street, near West Burnside Street. For hours and directions call (503) 227-5906 or visit www.danandlouis.com.

Above and Below

David Schargel can't help it. This former New Yorker and Hilton Hotel concierge is obsessed with Portland history and the Rose City's nooks, crannies, and curiosities. And lucky for us, he's made sharing what he's learned his full-time job.

The Portland Walking Tour has something for everyone, even gecko enthusiasts.

★ ★

Trivia

Strange Laws

Somehow, Portland Walking Tour guides have room in their brains for tidbits about things beyond the city limits, including these strange laws found on the Oregon books:

- In Oregon it is against the law to use canned corn as bait for fishing.

- In Oregon doughnut holes must be at least ⅛ inch in diameter.

- In Hood River it is against the law to juggle without a license.

- Salem has barred women's wrestling.

- In Marion ministers are forbidden to eat garlic or onions before delivering a sermon.

Schargel and his staff of equally fact-focused folks serve as the detail-oriented leaders of a variety of Portland Walking Tours that cover everything from the "Best of Portland" to its architectural oddities and epicurean delicacies. Follow them around town and you'll learn about Portland's plethora of quirky public art, its bevy of bridges, its cache of cast-iron columns, and its hold on microbrew history. They'll take you past a unique five-sided building, a statue that forecasts the weather, the World's Smallest Park, and a sculpture that, depending on the weather, once doubled as an informal car wash.

Curiosity seekers will be happiest on the scandalous Underground Portland tour, which travels the city's Old Town and Chinatown neighborhoods. The two-and-a-half-hour, 1.5-mile trek is filled with tawdry tales about the city's underground tunnels, its haunted basements and backrooms, its bawdy brothels, its gambling rings, and its notorious murders. While there are plenty of legends about these places, Schargel is quick to point out that so much of Portland's history is curious that he and his guides have no need to pass on legends, folklore, myths, rumors, or made-up ghost stories. "It's all real. And all really curious."

Portland Walking Tours start at the Visitor Information Center at Pioneer Courthouse Square (Southwest Sixth and Yamhill) in downtown Portland. For more information call (503) 774-4522 or go to www.portlandwalkingtours.com.

Ghosts at the Pizza Parlor

One of the stops on the Underground Portland walking tour is Old Town Pizza, a haunted restaurant built on the spot that once housed the lobby of the upscale, circa-1880 Merchant Hotel. Beneath the

There's no need to share your pizza with the resident ghost who left this memento.

★ ★

Sandy Jug

At one time this fun-to-encounter jug-shaped building at 7417 Northeast Sandy Boulevard had a multicolored billiards-themed paint job. The jug is still intact, but these days it's painted red and houses a bar and a strip club (The Pirate's Cove).

restaurant floorboards are the "Shanghai Tunnels" that some believe served as interconnecting underground pathways used to nab unsuspecting sailors and transport them to ships docked on the river that were in need of crew members.

But no floorboards, doors, or tunnels seem to deter the restaurant's resident ghost. "Don't be surprised," reads the restaurant menu, "if you feel a 'presence' behind you, smell a faint waft of perfume, or see a woman in a black dress heading down the stairs to the basement."

"That's just Nina," says the manager on duty the day we visited. "She's been here almost a hundred years, and we're pretty sure she's the one who carved her name in the bricks by the old elevator shaft in the back of the restaurant." Who was Nina? Legend has it she was a "working girl" at the Merchant Hotel who was found dead in the elevator shaft not long after agreeing to share information with traveling missionaries intent on cleaning up the neighborhood.

Old Town Pizza is located at 226 Northwest Davis. The "Nina" carving in the brick is viewable anytime the restaurant is open, but the tunnels down below are only accessible during private tours. For more information call (503) 222-9999 or visit www.oldtownpizza.com.

Top-Floor Justice

Portland police history is full of firsts. For example, in 1927 Portland was the first major police agency to report that 100 percent of its officers had completed the training academy course. And in 1932 the city was the first to install a police radio system.

But long before that, in 1905, Portland made the record books by hiring Lola G. Baldwin as the country's first policewoman. That

Those canine cops can sure take a bite out of crime.

year the city was hosting the Lewis and Clark Exposition, and rumor had it that many young girls had vanished during expositions back east. Officer Baldwin's job was to coordinate volunteers to meet all incoming trains and boats and ensure that innocent young women just arriving in town didn't end up in Portland's bawdy houses, which were notorious for recruiting "talent" among new arrivals. But Baldwin's job didn't end there: By 1908 she was superintendent of the entire Women's Protective Division.

Too bad Baldwin wasn't on duty the day in April 1874 when chief of police James Lappeus arrested fifteen members of the Women's Temperance and Prayer League for picketing downtown saloons. The women were charged with disorderly praying—a crime not found on the books then or now—and sentenced to one day in jail.

You can see the police blotter from that day at the Portland Police Museum. Other displays include a rapping, trench-coat-wearing mannequin of McGruff, the "Take a Bite Out of Crime" dog, and a collection of truly scary confiscated weapons, including a pipe bomb, various hatchets, and something that looks like a giant homemade wire whisk with a five-pound metal nut tucked inside.

The Portland Police Museum is on the sixteenth floor of the Justice Center at 1111 Southwest Second Avenue in downtown Portland. A photo ID is required for entry into the building. For more information call (503) 823-0019 or visit www.portlandpolicemuseum.com.

Hold On to Your Hat

When hat fancier Alyce Cornyn-Selby was house-hunting in Portland, she ended up moving into and eventually marrying (more about that later) the historic circa 1910 Ladd-Reingold House. It turned out to be a match made in hat heaven: The house had once belonged to Rebecca Reingold, a trained milliner from Russia.

Today the house is home to the country's only Hat Museum, and it's brimming with Cornyn-Selby's collection of more than 600 chapeaus. Make your way past the red leather 1966 Cadillac couch, the

Passing the hat takes on new meaning at the Hat Museum.
The Hat Museum/J. Alyce

bright red London telephone booth, and John Steinbeck's cast-iron lion doorstop and you'll see feathered Victorian hats, funny flowered hats, quirky costume caps, funky fedoras, and precious pillboxes. There are also military hats, cowboy hats, and a novelty hat section that includes headgear such as Wisconsin cheese hats, Hershey's Kisses hats, a tombstone hat, all sorts of animal hats, and a wide variety of hats with a food or holiday theme. The star attractions here are the giant teacup hat, the singing birthday cake hat, and the Thanksgiving table hat that requires the wearer to put their head right up inside the turkey.

Cornyn-Selby says she'd never ever leave the house without a hat, so she keeps a pile of her favorites by the back door. "I never have to worry about a bad hair day," says this author, motivational speaker, and self-taught hat maker. And she doesn't just collect hats. Her museum includes an assortment of more than a hundred hamburger-themed items (including a crossover hamburger hat) and a clothespin collection that includes a 10-foot example.

Cornyn-Selby is not only committed to her collections, she's committed to her house. Which is why, she says, she "married" it in 1966. "Well, we'd been living together for twenty years," she explains, "so I figured we had a good foundation. And I know there are studs in every room."

The Hat Museum is located in the historic Ladd-Reingold House in Portland's Ladd's Addition neighborhood and is open by appointment only. For reservations and directions, call (503) 232-0433 or visit www.thehatmuseum.com.

Parks R Us

With 37,000 acres of parkland, it's clear that Portland is serious about its green spaces. But in among the city's 288 parks are some with unusual attributes. Mount Tabor Park, for example, is actually an extinct volcanic cinder cone. Washington Park is home to the International Rose Test Gardens, the oldest continuously operated public rose test gardens in the country. And the five-and-a-half-acre Japanese Garden, with its five traditional gardens and authentic pavilion and teahouse, has been described as the most authentic Japanese garden outside of Japan. Portland's park system also includes the country's largest and smallest urban parks.

The largest is Forest Park, set in the hills above the city's Northwest neighborhood. The park's 4,873 acres contain more than 70 miles of interconnecting trails and lanes for hiking, biking, and running. A massive tree canopy and substantial undergrowth offer shelter to more than 112 bird and 62 mammal species, including elk, deer, and the occasional bear and cougar. The modern-day wildlife is similar to that noted by William Clark (of Lewis and Clark fame), who visited this area in 1806 on a side trip up the Willamette River. Clark had

Some say leprechauns live here.
Portland Parks and Recreation

★ ★

seen many of the animals before, but was impressed by the Douglas firs he found here: In his journal he mentioned seeing trees with trunks ranging from 5 to 8 feet in diameter.

While Forest Park overlooks the Willamette River near downtown, tiny Mill Ends Park is right in downtown. At only 24 inches in diameter, the country's smallest park has no trails, picnic areas, or restrooms, but it does have a colorful background, lots of fans and, some say, a resident colony of wee people.

The park was established—some say "invented"—in 1946 by local newspaper columnist Dick Fagan, who noticed that a light pole never arrived for a hole dug in the middle of a median strip near his office. Rather than watch weeds move in, Fagan planted flowers and dubbed the hole the "World's Smallest Park." He wrote columns about "events" held in the park, many involving the antics of the "only leprechaun colony west of Ireland."

Fagan died in 1969, but the park is still maintained. Over the years it's sprouted everything from tiny swimming pools and statues to miniature flying saucers. Events held on-site have ranged from picnics and band concerts to the occasional wedding. The 452-square-inch park is located at Southwest Naito Parkway and Taylor Street in downtown Portland and is marked by a sign that's notably larger than the park itself.

For more information go to www.portlandonline.com/parks/finder and use the drop-down list to find the parks, or call Portland Parks and Recreation at (503) 823-7529.

Pachyderm Party

Portland's zoo made international news in 1962 when it announced the birth of Packy, the first elephant born in the western hemisphere in more than forty years.

Even before he was born, Packy was a sensation. Portlanders got involved in a "Name the Baby" contest, stuffed elephants appeared in store toy departments, and for three months a zoo veterinarian

Packy arrives!
Oregon Zoo

lived in the elephant house, keeping a close watch on the maternity ward. When Packy finally arrived, on April 14, the birth of the 225-pound baby got an eleven-page spread in *LIFE* magazine as well as gifts from around the world, "everything from gold-plated safety pins to hand-knitted garments."

Now, at 13,500 pounds and 10 feet 6 inches at the shoulder, Packy is the largest Asian elephant in the United States. And every year the Oregon Zoo throws an elephant-size party for the city's favorite pachyderm. Packy gets a parade, presents, and a forty-pound whole-wheat birthday cake topped with frosting, apples, carrots, and celery. Yum!

The Oregon Zoo isn't just partial to Packy. It also has the largest breeding herd of Asian elephants outside their native jungles and

Oregon Zoo's Bear Beginnings

The Oregon Zoo traces its history back to 1887, when the mayor of Portland invited seaman-turned-pharmacist Richard Knight to move his two bears, Gracie and Brownie, into cages in a city park. Knight had been keeping the bears (a grizzly and a brown bear) staked outside his downtown drugstore, which at times also displayed parakeets, monkeys, and other small animals and birds.

the only elephant museum in the country. The circular Lilah Callen Holden Elephant Museum, located right next to the elephant compound, displays the skeleton of an 8-foot-tall, 13-foot-long mastodon thought to be more than 7,000 years old. The museum also displays a wide variety of unusual artifacts and historical items, including a circus elephant's giant red tricycle, a large howdah (saddle), artwork with an elephant theme, and an extensive elephant stamp collection.

The Oregon Zoo is open every day (except Christmas) and is located at 4001 Southwest Canyon Road, just west of downtown Portland on US 26. For more information call (503) 226-1561 or visit www.oregonzoo.org.

(Note: A great time to visit is on Two-Buck Tuesdays, the second Tuesday of every month, when admission is just $2 per person.)

Velveteria

Black velvet paintings. Of Elvis. Of naked ladies. Of John F. Kennedy, saucer-eyed puppies, or waves crashing against the shore. You've definitely seen them. Maybe in a bar or the lobby of a seedy motel.

★ ★

Or maybe you have your own favorite velvet painting hanging on your living room wall.

Don't be ashamed. Velvet paintings may have a corny, garish reputation, but the "art form" has been around for years. In fact, some trace its origins back hundreds or even thousands of years, to the times of Marco Polo and ancient Kashmir.

That may be true, but it wasn't the "fine art" angle that spurred Caren Anderson and Carl Baldwin to begin buying velvet paintings of clowns, kittens, devils, Republicans, cartoon characters, movie stars, dead presidents, and just about anything painted on velvet they could get their hands on. They just fell in love with velvet paintings and started buying them. Someone had to. "Velvet paintings are the Rodney Dangerfield of art," explains Baldwin, who says the pieces they found in thrift stores and antiques stores, on eBay, at garage sales and estate

This Black Velvet Elk would fit in well at the Velveteria.
Joe Myxter collection

★ ★

sales, and for sale on the sides of highways and in gas station parking lots range from fine art to "Oh my God, what were they thinking?"

When the collection topped more than a thousand velvet paintings, Anderson and Baldwin realized something had to be done. So they rented a storefront, picked 170 of their favorite paintings, hung them on the walls, and opened the Velveteria, a Museum of Velvet Paintings.

And it works. It's just one of those places you have to see and, in this case, feel to believe. There's a section of velvet paintings designed to be viewed under black light, a slew of banditos, and plenty of pieces that represent the "classics" of the genre, including naked ladies, dogs playing poker, religious icons, clowns, and images of the south seas. And just like a "real" art museum, there are regular themed gallery shows, such as the story of Jesus and Mary on velvet, Poodletopia, the Wild West, Clowntacular, and From Botox to Detox, which featured velvet scenes depicting the surgical evolution of Michael Jackson, the Three Faces of Kenny Rogers, and portraits of a variety of other celebrities.

The Velveteria is open Thursday through Sunday and is located at 2448 East Burnside. For more information call (503) 233-5100 or go to www.velveteria.com.

Here, Ribsy

"Henry Huggins was in third grade."

In 1950, Beverly Cleary started writing a children's book about a boy who wished that something exciting would happen to him. Cleary gave the boy a dog and named that dog Ribsy (short for Spareribs). Then she needed a good name for the street that young Henry would live on. No problem there: He'd live on fun-to-say-out-loud Klickitat Street, a real street in the Northeast Portland neighborhood where Cleary herself grew up.

Cleary's books about Henry Huggins and Ribsy were a big success. So were her stories about the adventures of Ramona Quimby, her

Cleary's storybook character Ribsy is ready to play.
Doug Sweet

older sister Beezus, and other characters Cleary created for a series of whimsical books that take place in Portland.

The books, and Ms. Cleary, went on to win worldwide recognition and just about every award possible. And in 1995, in a ceremony attended by Beverly Cleary herself, the characters of Henry Huggins, Ramona Quimby, and Ribsy the dog were immortalized with bronze statues in the Beverly Clearly Sculpture Garden in Portland's Grant Park. That park, the setting for many scenes in Cleary's books, is just four blocks from the real Klickitat Street.

In the garden, there are fountains under Ramona's and Ribsy's feet, which make it fun on a hot day. There are also granite plaques engraved with the titles of the books that take place in Portland. And for those who'd like to walk along Klickitat Street and see other spots where events in Cleary's books "really" took place, there's a stone map at the nearby Hollywood Public Library. The map marks seventeen landmarks, including Henry's paper route, Ramona's house, the

Ga-ga for Grant

Portland's Grant Park and Grant High School, as well as numerous streets, and both a town and a county in Oregon, are named in honor of Ulysses S. Grant, the country's eighteenth President.

Why is Oregon so ga-ga for Grant? As a member of the Fourth U.S. Infantry, Grant spent a year (from 1852 to 1853) at nearby Fort Vancouver, which was Oregon Territory when he arrived and Washington Territory when he left. While on assignment, he developed a soft spot for the area and hoped to someday come back here to settle down. He never did, but in 1879, after serving two terms as president, Grant and his family did came back for a much-publicized visit.

Colossal Market, and the new supermarket. Two homes where the young Beverly Clearly lived are also on the map.

The Beverly Cleary Sculpture Garden is just south of the playground in Grant Park, at Northeast Thirty-third Avenue at U.S Grant Place, next to Grant High School (Beverly Cleary's alma mater.) For directions and more information, see www.multcolib.org/kids/cleary/.

The Hollywood Public Library is at 4040 Northeast Tillamook Street. For directions, or to view the map, visit www.multcolib .org/agcy/hwd.html, or call the library at (503) 988-5391 for more information.

Rolling Along

Lots of cities have clearly-marked bike lanes these days and Portland is no exception. But in this quirky, bike-crazy city they just can't let those generic white bike-lane pavement stencils be.

Look down and you'll notice that, all over town, many of the basic bike-lane images have been altered. With some it's barely noticeable; with others it's hard to ignore. There's a police officer with a gun sticking out of a back pocket, a graduating student, a smoker, a cowboy (with a great pair of boots), bikers who are golfing, eating, and wearing all manner of silly hats.

How did they get there? And are they legal? Turns out that, about ten years ago, a city worker laying down bike-lane stencils added a funny little hat to one of the images just to see if his boss would notice. His supervisor actually liked the idea and soon bike-lane stencils were getting officially altered left and right.

The tradition has continued and today there are dozens of unique bike-lane pavement symbols all over town, including many with themes tied to their specific location, such as this bike rider found reading a book outside a library.

Bike lane stencils: read all about it
Doug Sweet

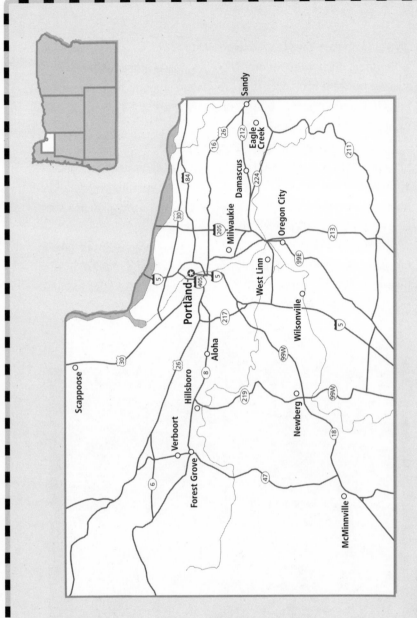

3

Greater Portland

*N*o need to stay within the Portland city limits to encounter things that are truly offbeat and out of this world. Out beyond the city limits we found a 26-foot-tall, 2,500-pound rabbit named Harvey, a 50-foot candle, one of the world's most unusual airplanes, and tales of a fifteen-ton visitor from outer space.

In Forest Grove ("Ballad Town"), we discovered the world's tallest barber pole. In Oregon City, we took a ride in the country's only outdoor municipal elevator. And in Wilsonville we pulled over to stretch our legs at a highway rest stop and ended up wandering through a mini-arboretum planted with the official tree from every state. And, perhaps to remind us of how important it is to eat well and exercise, out in front of an aquatic and recreation center in Hillsboro we met a jolly root beer and burger-hoisting family made up of statues that once graced A&W restaurants in the region.

★ ★

What's Up Doc?
Aloha

Ed Harvey's good-luck charm may be the rabbit's foot outside his boat shop in the Portland suburb of Aloha. Or it may be the almost 26-foot-tall fiberglass statue of a bunny man attached to it.

Harvey, the owner of Harvey Marine, says he first laid eyes on what would become his mascot back in the 1960s when a very large wind-damaged statue of a blue-jacketed Texaco gas station attendant was brought into the shop's fiberglass department. The repair estimate topped $2,000, so the owner abandoned the statue at the shop. Harvey let the big guy languish in the yard for a few years, then put him to work.

But not until the statue underwent some major cosmetic surgery.

Shop-owner Harvey was a big fan of the 1950 movie *Harvey*, starring Jimmy Stewart and an imaginary friend named Harvey, a 6-foot rabbit. "It was an uplifting movie," says Harvey the man. "Harvey the rabbit was sort of like an elf that keeps you out of trouble. So I decided to put a rabbit head on the fiberglass man and put him in front of my store."

Harvey, the 2,500-pound bunny-man, became an instant hit. And still is. Folks driving by wave and honk their horns. Many pull over to get their picture taken with the giant rabbit. He's become a popular meeting place and a landmark for those giving directions. ("If you get to the giant rabbit, you've gone too far.") And a holiday isn't official in town unless Harvey is celebrating with a Christmas tree, Halloween pumpkin, Thanksgiving turkey, Valentine heart, or American flag in his giant palm. "Once," says store manager Vicky McCurry, "he even had an old freezer in his hand decorated to look like a box of Girl Scout cookies." So far, though, Harvey hasn't celebrated Easter with an Easter basket. "It would be too expensive to make a giant basket for Harvey," says McCurry, "but I tell everyone he doesn't really need an Easter basket because he obviously *is* the Easter bunny."

Look up, Doc.
Allison George, Washington County Visitors Association

★ ★

Good enough. And who wants to argue the point with a 26-foot bunny-man anyway?

Look for Harvey outside Harvey Marine at 21250 Southwest Tualatin Valley Highway in Aloha. From US 26, head south on OR 217 (185th Avenue) and take OR 8 (Tualatin Valley Highway) west. Pull over when you see the giant bunny-man. For more information call (503) 649-5551 or visit www.harvey-marine.com.

Waxy Wonder
Damascus

Damascus celebrated the Oregon Centennial in 1959 with a gala fair and the fabrication of a giant Centennial Peace Candle. The 21-foot-tall, four-ton candle measured more than 3 feet across and was made locally out of chicken wire and welded-together pieces of cut-up old oil drums. Area children collected more than twenty tons of colored candle wax, which was melted down and then ladled into the giant empty mold. Lit on June 14, 1959, the candle burned for one hundred days at a rate of about an inch every thirty-six hours.

After the fair, the folks in Damascus decided that nothing could hold a candle to their melted Centennial Peace Candle except, well, another candle. So in 1962 a replica of the Peace Candle was placed in the park in downtown Damascus, right in front of the police station.

Firefighters don't have to worry about the flame from the candle setting anything ablaze. The "new" candle is made of steel and concrete and is covered in white stucco. According to civic booster Bob Rykken, although the stucco at the top of the cylinder is supposed to make it look like a melting candle, "it looks more like a white tube just sticking up out of the ground in the middle of the park than a candle. But the park is very nice."

The replica Centennial Peace Candle is located in downtown Damascus on OR 212, about 26 miles southeast of Portland.

The original Centennial Peace Candle.
Art Rykken

★ ★

Little World's Fair
Damascus

The 1962 World's Fair, also known as Century 21, was all about the wonders of the future. But while millions of people were flocking to Seattle, Washington, to get a glimpse of the world to come, the folks down south in Damascus, Oregon, were celebrating what no longer was.

Opened in June 1962 on twenty-two acres southeast of Portland, the Little World's Fair entertained visitors with stage shows, an old-style midway, a frontier town complete with a stockade, an Indian village with tepees, a blacksmith shop, a hotel, old City Hall, and a jail. To the delight of children and their parents, mock gunfights, shootouts, and bank robberies took place regularly, and folks could climb onto a stagecoach for a ride around the fair. And while Elvis and other top-drawer entertainers were stopping by the Seattle World's Fair, local groups such as the Damascus Frontiers offered western songs and other musical entertainment in the Little World's Fair saloon.

For dining, the 1962 Seattle World's Fair wowed diners up north with a motorized revolving restaurant that sat high atop the futuristic Space Needle. Not to be outdone, the Little World's Fair invited fair-goers to have a meal inside the Carousel, a circular, flag-festooned, ground-level restaurant that was kept in motion by a horse.

There's scant information to be found about the final days of the Little World's Fair. It's likely that the wooden storefronts of the mock frontier town were simply taken down and recycled, but rumor has it that the revolving restaurant did make its way to Seattle, where it was eventually sold for scrap.

Lasting Lilac
Eagle Creek

For many pioneers making the 2,000-mile trek west along the Oregon Trail, the Barlow Road linking the area between The Dalles and the Willamette Valley was the welcome "last leg" of the trip. But passage along the road wasn't free: When it opened in 1846, the fee to use the Barlow Road was $5 per wagon and 10 cents for each head of livestock. Those who couldn't pay the toll were free to turn around—or try their luck floating down the Columbia River to Oregon City instead.

Philip Foster arrived in Oregon Territory before the Barlow Road was built. He came by ship in 1843 and partnered with Sam Barlow to build the Barlow Road. Shortly after the road was built, Foster claimed land at

Brought from Maine in 1842, this is the oldest lilac tree in the state.
Philip Foster Farm

★ ★

the end of it—in Eagle Creek—and set up an early form of the modern-day "destination resort." Emigrants at the end of their long journey came over Mount Hood to find what many described in their diaries and letters as a "paradise" with hot cooked meals, a well-stocked general store, fresh fruits and vegetables, pastures for their stock, a blacksmith, camping sites, and cabins. Like the Barlow Road, however, nothing was free. Everything at Foster Farm was for sale or rent.

These days Foster Farm welcomes visitors for free (though there is a suggested donation). The well-groomed property has a replica of the original Pioneer Store, an apple orchard, flower and vegetable gardens, and the original 1860s barn. The farm is also home to Oregon's oldest lilac bush. Brought here from Maine by Philip Foster's wife, Mary Charlotte, the 160-plus-year-old lilac tree is still growing where she planted it in the 1840s.

The grounds of the Philip Foster Farm National Historic Site are open year-round, dawn to dusk. The buildings open on Father's Day in June and remain open daily through Labor Day; for the remainder of September, they are open only on weekends. The farm is located at 29912 Southeast OR 211 in Eagle Creek (five miles north of Esta-cada near the intersection of OR 211 and OR 224). For hours and more information, call (503) 637-6324 or visit www.philipfoster farm.com.

Camping Comfort
Eagle Creek Campground

Camping is a great way to experience the woodlands of the Colum-bia River Gorge. Many folks who find themselves at the Eagle Creek Campground in the Columbia River Gorge National Scenic and Rec-reation Area never learn about the site's historic claim to fame. But they probably make use of it.

According to the USDA Forest Service, the circa 1915 Eagle Creek Campground is considered to be the first Forest Service campground constructed in the United States. More importantly to campers seeking creature comforts in the woods, it's also the home of "Big John," the first restroom with flush toilets constructed in a Forest Service campground.

The Eagle Creek Campground is accessible from I-84 and is located 2 miles west of Cascade Locks, near Bonneville Dam. The campground is usually open May through September. For more information call (541) 308-1700 or search for Eagle Creek on the Columbia River Gorge National Scenic Area Web site: www.fs.fed.us.

Sake to Me
Forest Grove

Sake, the 6,800-year-old Japanese alcoholic beverage known in the West as rice wine, is made from rice, water, yeast, and koji, an enzyme that turns starch into sugar. While traditionally brewed like beer, sake is served and savored like wine and tastes best when it's fresh and made from the highest-quality rice and the purest water.

So in 1979 when an American sake lover wanted world-class sake, he decided to build his own sake brewery in the water-rich Pacific Northwest. The best spot for his sakery turned out to be Forest Grove, which sits at the edge of a lush rain forest aquifer on the east slope of Oregon's Coast Range.

Today SakeOne is the world's only American-owned-and-operated sakery. It produces four premium sakes and was the first to create a line of sakes with fruit-flavor infusions such as Asian pear, raspberry, and peach. Tucked into a region best known for wineries, SakeOne is open to the public every afternoon and offers complimentary twenty-minute tours of the sakery most afternoons.

It's a thoroughly modern facility, but traditional Japanese culture is not forgotten. Each March a Shinto priest from Portland stops by to perform a spiritual cleansing of the brewery building, or *kura*. And year-round a small shrine sits atop the computer panel monitoring the plant's production equipment as a reminder of the Japanese love of tradition, history—and modern technology.

★ ★

Old mixes with new at the sakery.
Ross Reynolds

SakeOne is located at 820 Elm Street in Forest Grove, just off OR 47 (Tualatin Valley Highway). For more information call (800) 550-SAKE or go to www.sakeone.com.

Shave and a Haircut

Forest Grove ·

Chuck Olson has been part of a barbershop quartet ever since he was a junior in high school. He's in his seventies now and still making harmony. And he still looks forward to singing in the Northwest Barbershop Ballad Contest that's been held every March in his hometown of Forest Grove, or Ballad Town USA, for the past sixty years.

Olson is such a barbershop quartet aficionado that when the Barbershop Harmony Society held its international convention and championships in Portland in 1973, he spearheaded a campaign to honor the event with the installation of the World's Tallest Barber Pole. "The conference had been in San Antonio several years earlier," says Olson, "and they put a 40-foot barber pole in front of the Alamo. At the time it was the world's tallest barber pole. I figured if treeless Texas can do that, we should be able to top them here in Oregon."

And they did. With a 70-foot pole, painted red, white, and blue, and a 2-foot-tall Styrofoam ball on the top, Oregon claimed title to home of the World's Tallest Barber Pole. "After the convention," says Olson, "we couldn't stand to just cut the pole up for firewood, so we arranged to bring it home to Forest Grove."

Today the World's Tallest Barber Pole stands next to a ball field in Lincoln Park. And while it's not an official site for any of the festivities surrounding the town's annual barbershop festival, lots of folks do come by to get their picture taken with the pole. Once in a while, they break into a barbershop ballad or two.

To reach Lincoln Park from Pacific Avenue in downtown Forest Grove, turn onto College Way and go around behind Pacific University to Sunset Drive. The World's Tallest Barber Pole will be in a parking lot by a ball field on the left-hand side.

The Northwest Barbershop Ballad Contest is usually held the first weekend in March. To confirm dates and location, and to get additional information, contact the Forest Grove Chamber of Commerce at (503) 357-3006.

It's no stretch to call this the world's tallest barber pole.
Ross Reynolds

A Night in Knight Hall

Legend has it that Knight Hall (the current admissions building at Pacific University in Forest Grove) is haunted by the ghost of a former student named Vera who died in the building. In addition to some sightings, there have been many reports of her singing, playing piano, and voicing displeasure at some students' performances. Each Halloween, during an event dubbed "A Night in Knight Hall," Pacific University students camp out in the building and attempt to communicate with Vera's ghost.

Exercise and Fries

Hillsboro

In the 1950s and 1960s, families just like this—made up of a mama, a papa, a baby, and a teen statue each hoisting a giant hamburger in one hand and a frothy, frosty mug of root beer in the other—stood in front of A&W Restaurants around the country. The fast-food chain, which began in 1919, now has almost 700 outlets around the world, but, alas, the beefy burger family mascots were retired long ago.

But in Hillsboro, family is family. So instead of letting these local burger buddies go bye-bye, the town adopted them and gave them a permanent and prominent home in front of the city's aquatic and recreation center. In 1983 the Hillsboro Planning Commission even designated the family an official Cultural Resource, ensuring that the Burger Family will be able to keep this home for the foreseeable future. "It's really fun to see the burger people each time I come here," said one young woman registering for her swim class, "and it's also an important reminder of why we should all get plenty of exercise."

★ ★

Nothing says "good buddies" like burgers and root beer.
Ross Reynolds

Hillsboro's Burger Family can be seen in front of the Shute Park Aquatic & Recreation Center at 953 Southeast Maple Street. The center is just off OR 8, which is also called the Tualatin Valley Highway or T. V. Highway. For specific directions call (503) 681-6127 or visit www.ci.hillsboro.or.us/ParksRec/SwimmingPrograms.

Spruce Goose
McMinnville

Before he was a weird, reclusive billionaire, Howard R. Hughes was an oil tycoon, movie producer, word-class aviator, and aeronautical engineer who set several aviation records during the 1930s. He may be most famous, though, for his role in bankrolling and building one of the world's most unusual airplanes: the Hughes Flying Boat

★ ★

H-4 (HK-1) Hercules, better known as the *Spruce Goose,* which now makes its home in Oregon.

During WWII shipbuilder Henry Kaiser joined with Hughes in a quest to develop giant "flying boats" that could move hundreds of troops and huge amounts of supplies across the Atlantic. Standard airplane materials such as steel and aluminum were in short supply, so Hughes decided to try to make the plane out of Duramold, an unusual wood product that was both strong and extremely light.

Hughes and Kaiser parted ways after the war, while the project was still incomplete and way over budget. Hughes stuck with it, investing more than $7 million of his own money, and on November 2, 1947, he startled everyone by flying the giant airplane a little over a mile at an altitude of 70 feet for about one minute.

Hughes had proven the giant wooden plane could fly, but for the

The *Spruce Goose* comes home to roost here.

★ ★

The *Spruce Goose* makes new friends.
Photos courtesy of Evergreen Aviation Museum

next thirty-three years the *Spruce Goose* remained in a sort of suspended animation. It never flew again, but Hughes paid more than
$1 million a year to keep the plane stored in a specially made hangar
and in flight-ready condition.

Greater Portland

★ ★

In 1976, when Hughes died, his holding company planned to take the plane apart and send pieces of it to aviation museums around the country. Instead the *Spruce Goose* stayed intact, and in 1983 was put on display in Long Beach, California, next to the RMS *Queen Mary*. In the late 1980s the Disney Corporation acquired the lease on the exhibit space and announced that the *Spruce Goose* had to go, so the historic airplane needed another home.

Aviation fans in McMinnville stepped in with a proposal to make the *Spruce Goose* the central exhibit in a brand-new museum. It took more than ten years, but after disassembly, packaging, transportation, reassembly, and refurbishing, the *Spruce Goose* was ready for viewing when the Evergreen Aviation Museum in McMinnville opened in June 2001. Today the *Spruce Goose* is on display in a giant building, alongside a Wright 1903 Flyer replica and more than fifty other historic aircraft, including a Russian Photon space capsule and a Lockheed SR-71A Blackbird.

The museum is located across OR 18 from the McMinnville Airport, about 3 miles southeast of McMinnville, at 500 Northeast Captain Michael King Smith Way. For more information call (503) 434-4180 or go to www.sprucegoose.org.

Out of This World
McMinnville

Since it first opened in 1905, the Hotel Oregon has served as everything from a restaurant, lounge, and dance hall to a bus depot, Western Union office, beauty parlor, and soda fountain. These days the homey, four-story historic hotel welcomes guests with a first-floor pub, pool tables, cellar and rooftop bars, and forty-two rooms named in honor of some of the more colorful characters who have worked and stayed here or who have lived nearby. Room 413, the Abigail Scott Duniway room, for example, is named in honor of the women's rights advocate who grew up in nearby Lafayette. Room 401, the Wayne the Singing Chef room, is named for the hotel cook who

129

★ ★

UFOs are unusual, but so are certain UPLs (Unidentified Panting Labs).
Sean McMenamin

doubled as the entertainment in the lounge in the 1950s. And Room 416, the UFO room, honors an infamous local 1950 UFO sighting.

Yup, the McMinnville area is home to what UFO experts consider to be one of the most compelling and authentic UFO sightings in history. Paul and Evelyn Trent claimed that on May 11, 1950, they made contact with aliens and photographed their encounter. Mrs. Trent reported that while feeding the rabbits in her yard in Dayton, about 11 miles from McMinnville, she noticed some "silvery discs" in the sky. She called for Mr. Trent to grab his camera, and he was able to snap two shots before the aliens took off in their flying saucer "at high speed, blasting the area with a power wind."

Today the town's link to alien infamy is celebrated and debated at the Annual UFO Festival held at McMenamins Hotel Oregon. It's the second-largest UFO festival in the country and includes presentations by a wide range of noted UFO experts, workshops on aliens and UFO-ology, screenings of alien-film favorites such as *ET*, an Alien Costume Ball, and a parade complete with marching bands and people and pets dressed to look like aliens. Or maybe they really are aliens . . .

The UFO Festival is held each May at the Hotel Oregon, located at 310 Northeast Evans Street in McMinnville. For more information call the hotel at (888) 472-8427 or visit www.ufofest.com.

Da Bomb
Milwaukie

From 1947 until 1991 this vintage World War II B-17G four-engine bomber served as shelter for a forty-pump independent gas station that was one of the top performers in the country. But before it became a quirky gas station landmark, the plane went through some incredible adventures. And so did its owner, Art Lacey.

After WWII Lacey decided that a retired war plane would be just the ticket to draw attention to his gas station just outside of Portland. He poked around a bit and found one to his liking, but it was in stor-age at the U.S. Air Force's Altus Air Base in Oklahoma. He headed east and bought the plane for $13,750, intending to fly it home.

There was one small problem, though: Lacey was an inexperienced flyer. Undaunted, he studied the manual while he taxied on the ground. And to get around the base flying requirements, he strapped a mannequin in beside him as a stand-in for a co-pilot.

Unfortunately, Lacey crashed. He emerged miraculously unscratched, but two airplanes, his and the one he slammed into during his landing, were a total loss. So "Lucky Lacey" and some friends simply got another vintage bomber and flew that one home during a raging snowstorm that made it, at times, impossible to see where they were going. Somehow, though, they did make it home to Oregon and landed at a small airport not far from Lacey's gas station.

Once on the ground, however, it proved harder to get the plane

★ ★

Fill 'er up.
The Bomber Complex

across town than it had been to get it across country. City officials wouldn't grant a permit to move the plane through the streets, so at 2 a.m. one Saturday morning, Lacey and some friends simply loaded the bomber on four trucks and drove it home. Along the way the plane was pulled over, but Lacey only received a $10 fine for moving a large load without a permit.

For years the bomber was a roadside attraction slowly deteriorating due to Oregon's climate, bird poop, and vandalism. But now restoration of the "Lacey Lady" is under way. Her nose is all shiny and new and on display inside the on-site WWII–themed Wings of Freedom Showcase, which is open Friday through Sunday from 10 a.m. to 2 p.m. (Admission is free.)

And while the gas station is long gone, you can still fill up your stomach at the memorabilia-packed Bomber Restaurant. It too has a

WWII theme, with a menu that includes Bomblettes (omelettes) and Bombarded Hash Browns for breakfast, and Tokyo Rose BLTs and Bomberburgers for lunch and dinner. There's even a souvenir shop that sells Bomber mugs, Bomber trading cards, Bomber alarm clocks, and other such items.

The Bomber Restaurant complex is located at 13515 Southeast McLoughlin in Milwaukie, southeast of Portland on OR 99E. For more information call (503) 654-6491 or visit www.thebomber.com.

High-Tech Housekeeping
Newberg

In the mid-1960s insatiable inventor Frances Gabe decided that she—and women everywhere—had much better things to do with their time than to spend it cleaning house. So she began working on a wide range of inventions for a house that would clean itself.

Word got out, and newspapers, magazines, and film crews came to call. Then, as Gabe tells it, "Women from all over the world called, crying and sobbing. Sometimes their husbands had to hold the phone for them, because they were so gosh-darn pleased that I had finally saved them from housework, they hated it so much."

Gabe was having nothing to do with traditional housework that involved getting out the pails and mops or getting down on hands and knees to wash the floors. Her self-cleaning alternatives include highly varnished hardwood floors that slope gently toward drains discretely placed in the corners, and sprinkler-style dispensers installed in the ceiling of each room. "Put in some soap, close the doors, turn on the sprinkler, and whoosh, the whole room is clean." Wondering about the furniture? "No problem there. I use boat varnish on all my wood furniture." What about the chairs and sofas? "Glad you asked. They're made with my patented waterproof upholstery."

Gabe seems to have thought of everything. There's a self-cleaning organic toilet, self-dusting book jackets, a combination dishwasher/

dish cupboard that eliminates the need to have both, and a "clothes freshener" designed to bypass washing machines.

Contacted on her ninety-first birthday in June 2006, Gabe had little time to chat. "I'm very busy these days working on new inventions." And she had a fresh frustration: "I've been forced to let a housekeeper in here twice a week because they think I can't get around so well anymore. Now I have to try to make different parts of the house messy so the housekeeper has an excuse to come and clean something in my self-cleaning house."

Squiggle City
Oregon City

They're ancient, oily, slimy, and ugly. They can grow up to 30 inches long and can weigh in at more than a pound. They've been around for more than 350 million years and have no true bones or jaws, but do have mouths lined with sharp, rasping teeth. Vitamin and protein rich, they're considered a delicacy in some parts of Europe, yet their tough and chewy meat is definitely an acquired taste. And although they look like eels and are commonly called eels, the Pacific lamprey is not an eel at all.

At one time millions of migrating lampreys joined salmon in an annual springtime journey up the Willamette River to spawn. Back

Earth Movers

According to the *Guinness Book of World Records,* the folks in Newberg set a world record on September 27, 2003, when 2,453 shovel-wielding supporters all dug simultaneously to break ground for the Providence Newberg Medical Center.

★ ★

Canned eels never really caught on.
Columbia Gore Discovery Center

then the eels so covered the Willamette Falls that it looked "like sea-weed had sprouted" out there.

For thousands of years these "wriggling masses of eels" were a staple in the diet of Native American tribes in the area, but while lampreys still swim up the Columbia River tributaries to spawn, their numbers are so small that steps have been taken to declare the lamprey an endangered species.

Going Up!
Oregon City

In 1915, after a great deal of political wrangling, Oregon City celebrated the opening of its outdoor elevator. Powered by 200,000 gallons of water each day, the elevator took about three minutes to travel 100 feet. For folks in town, though, that definitely beat the long climb up a set of rickety stairs that linked the older lower level of town along the river to the newer upper level at the top of the bluff.

In 1924 when the elevator was changed over to electric power, the ride up and down the hillside took just thirty seconds. And while today folks can easily drive from one part of town to the other,

The country's only outdoor municipal elevator has been operating since 1915.
Oregon's Mt. Hood Territory

Oregon City keeps its elevator staffed seven days a week and offers free rides to the public.

Why bother? Perhaps it's because the first U.S. city incorporated west of the Mississippi is intent on keeping its titles as the only city in North America with a "vertical street" (Elevator Street) and the only city in the country with an outdoor municipal elevator. (There are only three other such elevators in the world.)

Want a ride? The lower-level elevator entrance is in downtown Oregon City at 300 Seventh Street. Riders who start here are let out at a circular glass-enclosed observation area offering views of Oregon City and the Willamette River. Thanks to a recent major renovation project, a series of photographic, lenticular prints by artist Michael Asbill now grace the walls of the access tunnel, the elevator housing, and a spot beneath the observation deck windows. They allow viewers to see multiple 3-D pictures in the same image. The photos tell the story of pioneer migration and the development of the town. There is no charge to ride Oregon City's municipal elevator, which operates daily. For more information call (503) 657-0891.

Hamburger Heaven
Sandy

Got a hankering for a hamburger? It's a good bet you won't need to go far to find a McDonalds, a Wendy's, or a Burger King outlet. But for the past twenty years, fans of really big, really unusual hamburgers have been making regular pilgrimages out to Calamity Jane's Hamburger Restaurant, a gregarious, western-themed eatery known for its huge hamburgers and its long list of bizarre topping combinations.

Indecisive diners beware. The first order of business is choosing your hamburger size. There's the one-patty City Slicker, a dainty one-third of a pound. The two-patty Wrangler weighs in at two-thirds of a pound. And the three-patty Trail Boss tips the scales at a full pound of meat. For really hungry diners, or parties of eight or more, there's also a five-pound burger, which should be ordered forty-eight hours in advance.

That's the easy part.

Once you've decided on the size of your burger, it's time to choose the toppings. Sure, you can order a straight-ahead All American Burger with cheese, ketchup, lettuce, mayonnaise, tomatoes, onions, and pickles. But why bother making the trip for that when there are more than fifty other combinations on the menu? Like the George Washington Burger served with sour cream and hot, sweet, pie-worthy cherries. Or the Hot Fudge and Marshmallow Burger. Or any one of sixteen different types of pizza burgers, including a Pastrami and Pineapple Pizza Burger.

Nancy Nance has been a general manager at Calamity Jane's for more than five years and has had plenty of opportunities to sample some of the more unusual combinations herself. "My favorites? The Honey Lovin' Jimmy Carter Peanut Butter Burger and the Tijuana Temptation, a hamburger covered with taco meat, refried beans, tomatoes, onions, and lots of other stuff."

The original Calamity Jane's is located at 42015 Southeast OR 26 in Sandy (503-668-7817). It's a popular spot for skiers heading home to Portland from Mount Hood. For folks heading to the coast from Portland, a second Calamity Jane's is located at 1175 North OR 99 W in Dundee (503-538-9407).

Waxy Wonder
Scappoose

When they give directions to first-time visitors, all the folks in Scappoose need to say is, "Look for the giant red candle." And sure enough, if you're anywhere near Scappoose on US 30, you can't miss the 50-foot votive.

But why is it there? Are the folks in Scappoose afraid of the dark?

Nope, this megacandle was built in 1971 by a candle-making factory that had moved in at a local farm. To advertise their product,

Turn right at the candle.
Jeremy Jones

and no doubt just to see if it could be done, the company poured 45,000 pounds of wax over an unused silo and inserted a giant wick. The town's mayor and the state's governor came by to light the candle, using a specially made 60-foot-long match. Dubbed the Scappoose Peace Candle, the waxy wonder was dedicated in the name of world peace and was for a time listed in the *Guinness Book of World Records* as the World's Largest Candle.

In the rainy Northwest it's hard to keep any candle burning outdoors, let alone a 50-foot behemoth, so a gas flame was installed to illuminate the candle long term. But when the gas bill soared, the flame and the wax were replaced by more durable substances, including the neon "flame" that can now be seen from the highway. And depending on whom you ask, the Scappoose Peace Candle is either a giant red reminder to wish for world peace—or just a kooky, outsize remnant of someone's bright idea.

Pickled Party

Scappoose

Even though the Steinfeld's pickle and sauerkraut factory closed a few years ago, putting many locals out of work, the folks in the tiny town of Scappoose don't seem to be holding any grudges. In fact, everyone in town still looks forward to getting together for the annual Sauerkraut Festival, which has a different theme each year. In 2006, for example, it was a Sauerkraut Salute to Lewis and Clark and in 2009, a sauerkraut soup cook-off made for a "Souper Sauerkraut" theme.

The themes may change, but the elements of the festival remain pretty constant. There's entertainment, craft booths, the crowning of the Queen of Kraut, and the celebration of sauerkraut and its many uses.

How many uses could there be for sauerkraut? "More than you'd imagine," says festival organizer Lisa Smith. For starters, there's the popular sauerkraut ice cream made by the Lions Club. "The recipe is top-secret. All I can tell you is that it uses sauerkraut juice, which makes it a little tart." Also always quite popular, says Smith, are the chocolate sauerkraut cupcakes made by the area senior centers. "Sauerkraut, once you drain it, is just like zucchini, so it really tastes fine in cupcakes. Trust me."

Not convinced? Then perhaps you'd rather have a slice of sauerkraut pizza or one of the town's "world famous" sauerkraut sandwiches, made with sausage and smothered in sauerkraut and a slew of other condiments.

After watching a professional sauerkraut-making demonstration, the strong-of-stomach might want to enter the sauerkraut-eating

contest, where cash prizes are awarded to the first folks who finish piled-high plates of drained sauerkraut—with their hands behind
their backs. And then there's the cabbage-bowling competition,
which pits the local police department against the fire department in
a heated tournament for a trophy.

"We mangle a lot of cabbages doing that each year," says Smith,
"but don't worry; we don't use that cabbage to make any of our sauerkraut dishes. That cabbage is fed to the animals on a local farm."

The Scappoose Sauerkraut Festival is held each year on the third
weekend in September in downtown Scappoose, which is located 20
miles east of Portland on US 30. For more information contact the
South Columbia County Chamber of Commerce at (503) 397-0685
or visit www.sccchamber.org.

Sausage and Sauerkraut

Verboort

Once a year the folks in the small Dutch-Catholic farming community
of Verboort, just outside Forest Grove, invite folks over to the Visitation Parish for an all-you-can-eat sausage and sauerkraut dinner set
among a grove of giant sequoia (redwood) trees.

They've been holding their meat-eating marathon since 1934.
Back then 198 pounds of Dutch sausage and more than 10 gallons
of sauerkraut were served to 150 diners. By 2005 more than 7,000
hungry attendees were showing up to chow down on 13-plus tons
of smoked sausage and more than 2,300 gallons of sauerkraut made
from 10 tons of locally grown cabbage. And it's all ground, smoked,
baked, steamed, and cooked right there on church property.

Oh, and it's not just sausage and sauerkraut that gets dished out.
Every dinner comes with an array of side dishes, including salad, rolls,
mashed potatoes and gravy, green beans, and at least two kinds of
pie. To help wash it all down, there's a free shuttle bus over to the
beer garden at the nearby Verboort Rod and Gun Club.

For folks who, God forbid, don't get enough sausage on-site,

★ ★

there's a bulk-sausage sale and a drive-through window. As one reviewer said, "Forget about calories—you can do penance later . . . ."

Making you hungry? Verboort's Sausage and Sauerkraut Dinner is held each year on the first Saturday in November and is a fund-raiser for the parish school. In addition to dinner, there's bingo, a bake sale, and the ever-popular pot holder game, where prizes of small kitchen appliances, toys, and jewelry are awarded to those who purchase some of the "specially marked" handmade creations.

The dinner is held at the Visitation Parish, 4285 Northwest Visitation Road in Verboort, which is 3 miles north of downtown Forest Grove and about 23 miles west of Portland. For more information call (503) 357-6990 or go to www.verboort.org.

Dancers cavort with thirteen tons of sausage.
Annette Evans

Sauerkraut Cupcakes?

Don't knock 'em till you try 'em. These cupcakes sell like hotcakes at the Scappoose Sauerkraut Festival each year.

Surprising Cupcakes

⅔ cup butter

1½ cups sugar

3 eggs

1 teaspoon vanilla

½ cup unsweetened cocoa

2¼ cups sifted all-purpose flour

1 teaspoon baking powder

1 teaspoon baking soda

¼ teaspoon salt

1 cup water

1 cup sauerkraut, rinsed, drained, and squeezed dry

Preheat oven to 350 degrees. Thoroughly cream butter with sugar. Beat in eggs and vanilla. Sift together dry ingredients; combine with water until mixture is blended. Stir in sauerkraut. Pour into paper-lined muffin cups. Bake 15 to 20 minutes. When cool, frost with chocolate frosting.

Recipe adapted from Steinfeld's *Cooking with Kraut*, by the Scappoose–area Senior Centers.

Visitor from the Moon
West Linn

At fifteen-and-a half tons, the Willamette meteorite is the largest meteorite ever found in the United States and the sixth-largest meteorite in the world. And long before a Welsh miner found it in the Oregon woods, in what is now West Linn, the giant rock was considered a sacred object by Native Americans living in the Willamette Falls area. Back then the Clackamas people called it *Tomonowos,* which meant "Heavenly Visitor" or "Visitor from the Moon," and they believed the giant rock had mythical and spiritual meaning.

But the Clackamas people weren't around in 1902 when Ellis Hughes came upon the giant, egg-shaped chunk of iron and nickel on property owned by the Oregon Iron and Steel Company. Hughes recognized the rock as a meteorite and decided he just had to have it. So over the course of more than three months, he secretly worked to dig up the meteorite, build a road, and drag the rock home. Hughes then built a shed over the meteorite and charged people 25 cents to come take a gander at the pockmarked wonder.

Not long after Hughes set up his roadside attraction, however, the Oregon Supreme Court made him give the meteorite to the company that owned the land he'd taken it from. In 1905 that company put the meteorite on a barge to Portland so that it could be put on display at the Lewis and Clark Exposition. After the exposition the meteorite was sold to a Mrs. William Dodge for $20,600. She donated the space rock to the American Museum of Natural History in New York, which now displays the meteorite in the museum's Rose Center for Earth & Space.

Over the years Native American tribes in Oregon have made attempts to bring the meteor back home to the Willamette Valley. Although those efforts haven't been successful, in 2000 the museum and the Confederate Tribes of the Grand Ronde Community of Oregon signed an agreement that allows the museum to keep the meteorite on display but permits the Grand Ronde people to make an annual ceremonial visit.

Miss the Meteorite?

The real Willamette Meteorite may be staying in New York City, but replicas—of sorts—remain in Oregon.

In West Linn there are two meteorite memorials. A large one (which looks nothing like the original meteorite) stands near the Willamette United Methodist Church at the corner of Willamette Falls Drive and Fourteenth Street (1683 Willamette Falls Drive). A smaller, more correctly shaped version is displayed inside the West Linn Chamber of Commerce offices at the Postal Annex at 2020 Southwest Eighth Avenue. For information call (503) 655-6744 or visit www.westlinnchamber.com.

A more "meteor-like" copy of the meteorite sits outside the University of Oregon's Museum of Natural and Cultural History in Eugene at 1680 East Fifteenth Avenue. The museum also owns a small piece of the real Willamette Meteorite, which it keeps in storage.

Folks intent on seeing a piece of the real rock from outer space in Oregon will be happy to know that a 7.5-inch, 4.5-ounce chunk of the Willamette Meteorite is on display at the Evergreen Aviation Museum in McMinnville. For more information call (503) 434-4180 or go to www.sprucegoose.org.

★ ★

Tree-mendous
Wilsonville

The Baldock Rest Area on the south side of I-5 near Wilsonville is the largest and most visited rest stop in the state. More than 3,300 cars stop here each day, which tallies up to more than a million vehicles a year.

No doubt the folks in those vehicles are pulling over mostly to use the restrooms, stretch their legs, consult their maps, or walk their dogs. But those who take a few minutes to look around are often surprised to discover a well-tended, fifty-three-tree mini-arboretum with descriptive signs in front of each tree.

The project began in 1967 as the brainchild of then-state attorney general Robert Y. Thornton. He wanted to do something lasting in

Find your state tree.
Ross Reynolds

honor of the National Association of Attorneys General, an organization whose annual meeting was being held that year in Portland. So he arranged for the State Highway Department (now the Oregon Department of Transportation) to plant the official tree of each state (plus Guam, Puerto Rico, and the Virgin Islands) along a circular pathway at the Baldock Rest Area.

Today a walk through the Grove of the States is a journey along a shaded, restful, educational, and, at times, puzzling path. Oregon (tree number forty-eight) is represented by a Douglas fir. A Sitka spruce stands tall for Alaska (number forty-five), and there's a double-trunked giant sequoia here from California (number forty-six). But some of the trees planted here are no longer their state's official tree. Others never were. For example, in 1972 the cottonwood replaced the American elm as Nebraska's state tree, but the American elm still represents that state in the grove. The Japanese pagoda tree stands in for the official trees of Hawaii, Guam, Puerto Rico, and the Virgin Islands because trees from these locales are not hardy in Oregon. And all that's left of the Arkansas pine at spot number eighteen is a sad, lonely stump.

The Grove of the States is located near the picnic tables to the right of the restrooms at the Baldock Rest Area on the south side of I-5, near milepost 282. It's about 25 miles north of Salem and 19 miles south of Portland.

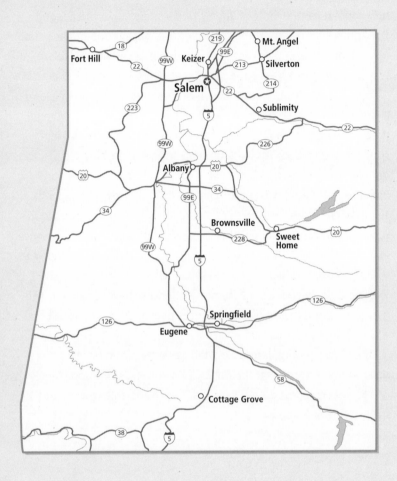

Willamette Valley

4

Willamette Valley

*T*his part of Oregon encompasses oh-so-serious Salem (the state's capital) and thousands of acres of fields filled with grapes, berries, and more than 250 other crops. The Willamette Valley is also home to the annual Jell-O Art Show in artsy, left-leaning Eugene, where you can see the World's Oldest Sandals and the waffle iron used to cook up the first Nike sneakers, and attend an annual slime-induced ceremony to crown the town's newest Slug Queen. A cache of curiosities await you in Mt. Angel. The Bavarian-themed town has built the world's largest glockenspiel, which sports a 49-foot tower with action on several levels. And right up the road, at the Mount Angel Abbey, Benedictine monks watch over a museum filled with what one monk charmingly calls "collectobelia": taxidermied animals, ships in bottles, fossils, and a wide variety of oddities of nature, including what certainly must be the World's Largest Hairball.

★ ★

Foam Home
Albany

Steve Fletcher, owner of Sprayfoam, Inc., in Albany, has been working in the insulation business for more than twenty-five years. He usually works on boats, tanks, and homes, but over the years he's created dozens of spray-foam works of advertising art, including a 37-foot whale in Alaska, giant jackalopes and dinosaurs in Wyoming, and a variety of larger-than-life foam statues that include a 14-foot duck, a family of opossums, and a miner and his burro, all here in Albany.

But Fletcher's most personal and perhaps best-known spray-foam creation is his own foam-covered home. "I started with a flat,

This spray-foam duck now roosts indoors.
Jimmie Lucht

concrete office building that just had no class," says Fletcher, who also runs his business out of this building, "so I decided to use left-over insulation materials to transform the roof into a foam volcano. Then I added some decorative landscaping, including a 5-foot lava flow around my property, some waterfalls, and a trout-stocked foam pond with a viewing window." The volcano, once open to the sky, is now a closed rooftop mountain, complete with a 20-foot hot tub made from spray foam. "Being single," says Fletcher, "I have a lot of latitude with my home decoration, so I can do what I want."

Fletcher says visitors are welcome to feed the trout in the pond, but please, no fishing. For directions to the foam home and other spray-foam creations in Albany, see the upcoming "Find the Foam" driving-tour sidebar.

Turn Right When You See the Opossum

Albany

When Jim Stauble opened his auto-body repair shop back in 1981, there were a lot of wild opossums in the area. "People were always running over them," says Stauble, "so when we needed a name for the shop that would stick in people's minds, we decided to call it Possum." To help get the point across, Stauble hired the local spray-foam company to put a giant cartoonlike statue of an opossum on the roof of his original shop. Later, when he moved the shop into a larger building, the 7-foot-tall opossum statue was placed by the side of the road, and soon three cute opossum babies appeared in a nearby tree.

Over the years the opossums have become town landmarks. Locals and tourists stop by to get their picture taken with the opossums, especially during the holidays when the cute critters get dressed up, donning Santa hats for Christmas, waving flags on July fourth, and feasting on a turkey dinner at Thanksgiving.

"It's kind of dumb," laughs Stauble, "but it works. Everyone—even little kids who don't drive—knows the name of our shop."

★ ★

Opossums help make this auto-body shop a local landmark.
Jimmie Lucht

The statue of the giant opossum and her three babies can be seen at Possum Autobody and Paint at 136th Ninth Ave SW. Be sure to go by when the shop is open; the opossums are made of lightweight material and are wheeled in at night.

Find the Foam

Once you see one of Albany's spray-foam attractions, you'll want to see them all. So call ahead to the Albany Visitors Association at (541) 928-0911, e-mail them at info@albanyvisitors.com, or stop by their information center in the Two Rivers Mall downtown at 250 Broadalbin Street. They will be more than happy to give you specific directions to the foam house at 430 Northeast Geary Street, the 14-foot foam duck inside the antique store at 131 Montgomery Avenue, the foam opossums at 136th Ninth Avenue SW, the miner and the burro at the South Pacific Auto Lot at 5050 Pacific Boulevard SW, and the foam eagle north of town.

This foam eagle hangs out north of town.
Oliver Anderson

Better Than a Hole in the Ground

Albany

In 1848 founders Walter and Thomas Monteith named this Willamette Valley town after their home state capital of Albany, New York. The name stuck until 1853, when some residents persuaded the Territorial Legislature to adopt the name Takenah, which was the word used by the local Kalapuyan tribe to describe the deep pool at the meeting point of the Calapooia and Willamette Rivers.

Unfortunately, the popular translation of Takenah was "Hole in the Ground," a description that embarrassed some of the residents of what was fast becoming an up-and-coming city. Bowing to pressure, the legislature discarded the Takenah moniker in 1855, and the name Albany was reinstated.

Today Albany has three historic districts listed in the National Register of Historic Places. It also has four fire stations and a team of paid firefighters. But in the late 1800s the city had an all-volunteer fire department and no money to buy equipment. To raise funds, roll call was taken after every fire. Volunteers who showed up to help fight the fire were asked to put 25 cents into the department coffers. Volunteers not present at roll call were dunned 50 cents.

For more information about Albany, including information on a self-guided walking or driving tour, call the Albany Visitors Association at (800) 526-2256 or go to www.albanyvisitors.com.

Biblical Beauties

Brownsville

In 1962 after ten years of convalescing from a disabling illness, former surveyor and forester Howard Taylor rose up from his sickbed and, like a man possessed, began toting the rocks and cement he needed to build his circular, gemstone-studded Living Rock Studios. He wanted a place to house his art, which includes a series of biblically inspired stone paintings, extraordinary wood carvings, more than a hundred oil paintings of birds and other wildlife, and an assortment

One of Howard Taylor's translucent stone masterpieces.
Jayna Bergerson

of family antiques reaching back to the pioneer days.

Many people come to see Taylor's carvings of dozens of different types of Oregon woods transformed into tiny working versions of hand tools, such as different types of pliers, and other items like a curling iron and a pocket knife, each with moving parts. But by far the main attractions here are Taylor's seven, brilliantly-colored Living Rock Pictures depicting Bible scenes such as Moses and the Burning Bush, the Nativity, and Joseph walking into Egypt.

Taylor, who died in 1996, made these intricate scenes by feverishly sawing, polishing, and gluing together hundreds of extremely thin pieces of agate and other rocks. He then carefully placed each over-size translucent stone picture into its own darkened nook so that the image could glow when lit from behind.

In the center of Living Rock Studios is Taylor's Tree of Life, a 30-foot-tall hollow structure made of pieces of petrified wood. Inside the tree a curved stairway studded with crystals leads to a second floor. "Daddy didn't want anyone touching his crystals," says Taylor's daughter Nancy, "but I've tried and you can't pull them off. So now I hand people flashlights and tell them to just enjoy."

Living Rock Studios is located at 911 Bishop Way (OR 228) just east of the city limits of Brownsville. Look for the petrified tree by the side of the road. Call ahead for hours at (541) 466-5814 or go to www.livingrockstudios.org.

Toga! Toga! Toga!
Cottage Grove

Like a student cramming for finals after a semester of skipping classes, the classic, wacky college-comedy film *National Lampoon's Animal House*, starring John Belushi, was shot on location in Oregon during just thirty-five rushed days in 1977. The movie, which was produced for only $3 million, was deemed "culturally significant" by the United States Library of Congress in 2001 and added to the list of films preserved in the National Film Registry.

Many locations in and around Eugene had bit parts in the movie, but the folks in nearby Cottage Grove don't want anyone to forget that the film's now-famous parade scene was filmed in their town.

Back in 1977 hundreds of locals happily donned togas and marched down Main Street as extras in the film. And for many years there was an annual reenactment of the parade, complete with re-creations of floats from the movie, during an Animal House Celebration and Toga Party. The first year's reenactment was so well attended, in fact, that the 2,166 participants established a Guinness World Record for the World's Largest Toga Party.

Food fight anyone?

Cottage Grove is located off I-5 at exit 174, about 20 miles south of Eugene.

There's Gold in Them Thar Hills
Cottage Grove

Sometime around 1863 gold was discovered just east of modern-day Cottage Grove in an area known as Bohemia Mountain, named for James "Bohemia" Johnson. Within a few years the area had a bustling town with homes, stores, a hotel, and, of course, saloons. The late 1800s and early 1900s were bonanza days for the area: Nearly 2,000 gold claims were filed, but most mining activity died down by the 1920s.

These days there are just a few active mining claims, but folks around Cottage Grove still mine the region's gold-mining past at the Bohemia Gold Mining Museum at 724 Main Street. Exhibits include mining tools, mine and claim maps, and examples of "fool's gold"—minerals that look like gold but are, sadly, pretty much worthless.

The area's gold-tinged past is also celebrated the third weekend in July, during the annual Bohemia Mining Days festivities. Events and activities include mining displays, the Grand Miner's Parade down Main Street, a street dance, and the re-creation of a gold-mining town at Coiner Park, just a few blocks from downtown. Each year

★ ★

Portrait of a miner at work.

about 1,000 folks also make the forty-five-minute drive out of town and up the one-way gravel road to Bohemia Mountain, for an "old time" miner's breakfast. For more information call (541) 942-5064 or go to www.bohemiaminingdays.org.

Buster's Back

Cottage Grove

Silent-film star Buster Keaton—famous for writing, directing, and producing his own films—came to Cottage Grove in 1926 to shoot what would become one of Hollywood's most famous scenes.

The fifteen-second shot was incredibly dangerous and was, at the time, the most expensive shot ever attempted. But Keaton wanted authenticity, and rather than create a cheap model, he spent $40,000 to build a real train trestle to nowhere, just so he could set it on fire and dump a locomotive off of it.

The movie was *The General*, and it was based on an actual American Civil War incident in which a Southern train engineer, played by Keaton, uses a locomotive named the *Texas* to chase after northern spies who have hijacked the *General,* his beloved train.

Keaton filmed the scene on the Row River, in the Culp Creek area about 16 miles east of Cottage Grove, in front of a crowd of onlookers that swelled to more than twice the town's population. Unfortunately, not everyone in the crowd knew that the train that crashed was full of dummies. "One woman was firm in her belief that both engineer and fireman had been killed," reported the local paper.

Buster Keaton's 1926 filming of *The General* is remembered year-round.

For years the leftover, mangled trestle, the locomotive, and the steel rails from the movie served as a local tourist attraction, but in 1941 those items were gathered up for scrap metal. Left behind was one rusted iron rail that, to this day, no one can seem to remove from the river bottom.

That rail, the Cottage Grove Hotel (where Keaton stayed), a Keaton mural at Ninth Avenue and Main Street, and spots around town that served as background for Civil War battles and other scenes, still draw visitors. This is especially true during the town's annual Buster Keaton Day, held each October, when film fans from around the country show up for tours, lectures, visits with Keaton relatives, and screenings of *The General* and other Keaton classics. For more information call (541) 942-2411 or visit www.cgchamber.com.

Opal's Aura
Cottage Grove

Some say she was a genius who could commune with the animals in the woods. Others called her a fake and a fraud. But for a while during the early 1900s, Opal Whiteley was Oregon's most famous writer. Today she's mostly misunderstood.

A daughter in a logging family that settled in Cottage Grove, Whiteley was a precocious child who began keeping a diary at age five. Described as a prodigy, she enchanted those around her and seemed to have a special, magical connection with plants and animals.

In 1920 the Atlantic Monthly Press published what was purportedly Whiteley's childhood diary. The best-selling book caused a sensation worldwide with adults and children who thought it a charming account of a young girl's observations about the world and her descriptions of mystical adventures with creatures from the woods. Later, however, the diary was labeled a fraud, and Whiteley's claims to being a princess with long-lost connections to French royalty were widely discredited.

"Princess" Opal still reigns over Cottage Grove.
Brianna Caridio

Looking back, some suspect Whiteley may have been suffering from undiagnosed schizophrenia, but back then her incessant claims to royal status and other odd behavior got her locked up in a British mental institution. She died there in 1992, well into her nineties.

The fascination with the Opal Whiteley saga has never really died down. Books and articles continue to be written about her, and there have been plays and a Broadway musical based on her life's adventures. And in Cottage Grove "Princess" Opal is remembered with a statue at the Cottage Grove Public Library (700 Gibbs Avenue) and, nearby, a block-long mural overlooking a small park on Main Street.

Eugene Eccentricities

- Eugene was the first city in Oregon to have one-way streets.

- Eugene is the home of Oregon's largest publicly-owned electric utility, the Eugene Water & Electric Board. It got its start in 1911, after a typhoid epidemic was traced to the groundwater supply.

- Jack Nicholson's "hold the chicken, bring me the toast" scene in the 1970 movie *Five Easy Pieces* was filmed at a local Denny's restaurant.

- The annual nonprofit Oregon Country Fair is a three-day, hippie-style music and crafts gathering that began in 1969 and now takes place every summer in Veneta (13 miles west of Eugene). Over the years it's turned into one of the largest volunteer events in the country and draws more than 50,000 people. During those three days the festival becomes one of the largest cities in Oregon—and definitely the city where the residents are having the most fun.

- Eugene is the birthplace of Nike. The waffle iron used to create the original versions of the company's legendary footwear is on display, along with many other company artifacts, at the Nike Store and Heritage Wall at 248 East Fifth Avenue, in the Fifth Street Public Market.

Art or Dessert?

Eugene

To most of us, it's simply a colorful, often bland dessert. Or a food associated with being sick or in the hospital. But to the performance artists in Eugene who call themselves the Radar Angels, Jell-O is inspiration for weird art.

For the past eighteen years this group has been holding an annual Jell-O Art Show that's become so popular, *Reader's Digest* named it the "Best Funky Food Show." Held each year at the Maude Kerns Art Center, this famously wiggly food show features ephemeral and permanent art made from Jell-O or similarly-textured gelatinous substances. Inspired by the medium, event organizers admit that they define "art" very loosely.

Art supplies for the Jell-O Art Show.
Ross Reynolds

163

★ ★

So you never quite know what to expect. Past entries have included Jell-O landscapes, lampshades, and hairdos; hats and other articles of jiggly Jell-O clothing; and a wide variety of surreal, shaky sculptures. And while the work ranges from silly to high concept, it's not uncommon for "technical issues," such as sunshine or slippery transportation conditions, to change the form of an entry on its way to the show.

With all that quivering, colorful art, an art patron can get hungry. So the Radar Angels ensure there's always a buffet laden with Jell-O-based dishes such as hand-dipped chocolate-covered brussels sprout "truffles" or Jell-O sushi. It sounds scary, but event organizers say the food table is always empty by the end of the night.

The Jell-O Art Show is usually held in early April, often on April 1, at the Maude Kerns Art Center in Eugene at 1910 East Fifteenth Avenue. For more information call the center at (541) 345-1571 or visit www.mkartcenter.org/events.htm.

Royal Gastropod
Eugene

In a city known for rampant individualism, non-conformity and occasional political divisiveness, Eugene's Slug Queen serves as an unofficial city ambassador and a slimy symbol of unity.

Each year since 1983, judges (who are all former or, as they're officially known, "old" Slug Queens) gather to shine the slimelight on a new queen to represent S.L.U.G., the Society for the Legitimization of the Ubiquitous Gastropod.

Contestants in the offbeat, end-of-summer pageant are rated not on their beauty and poise but on their costumes (the campier and more slug-like the better), their performances (the wackier the better), and their wits (the snappier and sassier the better). Unlike more formal, traditional pageants held elsewhere, those vying for the title of Slug Queen are allowed (and, in fact, strongly encouraged) to bribe the judges, who as past title-holders, know all too well the

One of Eugene's former, or more properly, "old," Slug Queens.
Travel Lane County

value of a well-greased palm. (Hint: If you're thinking of entering the Slug Queen contest, word on the street is that slug-themed pizza, chocolate, or wine will often do the trick.)

As for the duties of the Slug Queen, he (yes, men can and have held the title of Slug Queen) or she presides over the annual Eugene Celebration parade, makes appearances at ribbon-cutting ceremonies, art shows, cultural festivities, and other local events, and generally does their queenly best to exude free-spirited slime around town.

The Slug Queen contest and coronation is held each year in early September during the annual Eugene Celebration. For more information ooze on over to www.slugqueen.com.

★ ★

Just Ducky

Eugene

Before 1909, when Oregon adopted the Beaver State nickname, it was known as the Webfoot State. Although forward-thinking on most things, students at the University of Oregon rejected the modern motto and stuck with the old nickname, referring to themselves as Webfooters and to their athletic teams as the Ducks.

In fact the school's first live mascot, adopted in the early 1920s, was a duck (actually a succession of ducks) named Puddles, who waddled his way through campus games until the 1940s, when complaints from the Humane Society and others nixed the practice.

In 1947 folks at the school were still pining for a plucky, Puddles-like presence. That's when the school's athletic director, Leo Harris, made a deal with Walt Disney. Not Disney the company; Disney the man. Harris and Disney struck a deal that allowed the university to become the first—and only—school to use the likeness of Donald Duck as a mascot. The one restriction: It had to be done in good taste.

The unusual deal was made even more unusual in that it was closed with just a handshake. Back then that was good enough, and for about twenty years Walt Disney Productions generously sent along drawn versions of the famous duck for the university to use on athletic gear. But then Disney died in 1966, and both parties realized there was nothing to prove that the university really had a right to use Donald Duck's image.

Walt Disney wasn't around to confirm the deal, and there was no paper contract. But the university had something that turned out to be just as good or better: a photograph showing Mr. Disney wearing an Oregon letterman's jacket with Donald Duck on the front. That was good enough for the Disney lawyers, and an official contract was drawn up in 1973 that allowed the school to continue using Donald Duck as its mascot.

The ducky relationship was cemented even further in 1984 when Donald Duck turned fifty and stopped by Eugene for a visit. Close to 4,000 fans showed up to greet him at the airport, and the distinguished duck was presented with an academic cap and gown and named an honorary alumnus of the University of Oregon.

Donald Duck was the only duck mascot in any collegiate or professional capacity until 1993, when the Anaheim Mighty Ducks came on the scene in the National Hockey League. However, the University of Oregon remains the only institution ever licensed to use the image of Donald Duck as its mascot.

All Wound-up

Eugene

Back in 2005 Eugene resident Steve Milton and his sons embarked on a fun, family project that would end up stretching their imaginations—and more than 175,000 rubber bands.

All wound-up and ready to roll, this rubber band ball from Eugene was once the world champion.
OfficeMax

★ ★

After reading about John Bain, the Wilmington, Delaware man who'd set a Guinness World Record in 2003 with his 3,100 pound rubber band ball, Milton and his sons decided they'd try to beat that record with their own big, bouncy creation. They began working on their project in the house, but soon rolled it out to the garage where they ended up with a rubber band ball that was 5½ feet tall, 9 feet in circumference, and 4,594 pounds.

The rubber band ball was big all right, but to attain championship status it needed official confirmation. So in November 2006, with the help of a company whose corporate icon is a rubber band ball (OfficeMax), the Milton's rubbery sphere was transported to downtown Chicago. There, an official from Guinness World Records conducted an official weigh-in and declared a new winner in the Largest Rubber Band Ball Category.

Since then, the Milton's champion rubber band behemoth has toured the country and appeared at a wide variety of promotional events. And while it's famous far beyond its birthplace of Eugene, this record-breaking rubber band ball is no longer the world's biggest. In November, 2008, Joel Waul snatched that title away with a 9,032 pound rubber band ball that is more than 6 feet tall and made from more than 700,000 rubber bands.

World's Oldest Shoes
Eugene

Think you may have the world's oldest shoes kicking around in the back of your closet? Not even close. At the University of Oregon's Museum of Natural and Cultural History there's a pair of sandals that are 10,000 years old. Woven out of sagebrush bark by native people of southeastern Oregon, these sandals were discovered in 1938 by Dr. Luther S. Cressman in Fort Rock Cave in the Great Basin region of Oregon's high desert.

Tom Connolly, the museum's director of research, is confident that the sandals constitute "the oldest known shoe collection in the

You really don't know somebody until
you've walked in their shoes.
Dr. Thomas Connolly

world." He goes on to say, "There were parts of a hundred or so sandals found in Fort Rock Cave, and dozens more similarly made sandals
were found in several other northern Great Basin caves." And while
Connolly says all of the "Fort Rock–style" sandals the museum has
dated are somewhere between 9,300 and 10,000 years old, there's
no way of telling for sure if back then they were the latest style.

In addition to those old shoes, the museum displays a traditionally-
made wikiup (a pole-framed hut), a replica of a coastal plank-house,
and other items from its collection of more than a million artifacts
relating to the cultural history of the Northwest.

Got something in your closet you think may be as old as the
Fort Rock sandals? Don't throw them out just yet. The museum
has an annual Identification Day when experts in basketry, bones,

archeology, local history, textiles, and more are on hand to help
name and date strange objects.

The University of Oregon's Museum of Natural and Cultural History
is located on the university's campus, at 1680 East Fifteenth Avenue
in Eugene. For more information call (541) 346-3024 or go to www
.uoregon.edu/~mnh/.

Yard-o-Fun
Fort Hill

There are some strange things growing in Tim Tharp's yard. And
thank goodness he's got a really big yard and a really great wife who,
after first getting alarmed at her husband's definition of "art," told
him, "Well, let's not sweat the small stuff."

This is just one example of Tim Tharp's unusual yard art.
Salem Convention and Visitors Bureau

★ ★

So he hasn't. Out on the front lawn there's a 25-foot-tall martini glass. A yellow submarine. A 20-foot-tall Route 66 sign, and an equally large Statue of Liberty. Up in a tree there's a red, white, and blue pickup truck.

"It started with that martini glass," says Tharp, who works out of his home as a lumber broker. "I saw it, bought it, put it on the lawn. After that I just kept going. I can't tell you why."

Who cares why? Certainly not the curious folks who pull off the side of the road just outside Fort Hill, marveling at the stuff in front of the white house with the green roof. "It's become a roadside attraction," says Tharp's mother-in-law. "People take pictures, and everyone knows the holidays have arrived when Tim turns on the hundred or so lights he has hanging on that martini."

The Tharp Farm is located just east of Fort Hill, near milepost 26 on OR 18 and the intersection of OR 22, about 30 miles west of Salem.

On the Line
Keizer

The 45th parallel is an imaginary line that circles the earth at a spot halfway between the equator and the North Pole. It sweeps its make-believe way right across Oregon, and while some may say it's merely a line on a map, many towns and cities that straddle that line fully embrace their longitudinal position on this geographically significant halfway point.

The folks in Lincoln City, Salem, North Powder, and Fossil, for example, have put up roadside signs alerting travelers that they've reached the 45th parallel. But outside of Salem, officials in suburban Keizer have been contemplating a way to honor that town's parallel position with something more significant.

For a while the plan was to paint a yellow line across the road where the 45th parallel passes through town. "But we realized a stripe across the road would just confuse drivers, make them slow

★ ★

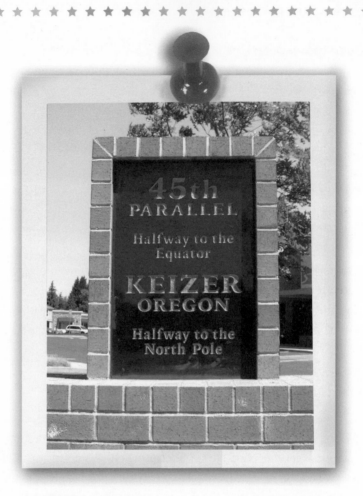

Cities on the 45th parallel are proud of their "parallel-ness."
Keizer Chamber of Commerce and Visitors Center

down, and probably cause accidents," says one parallel promoter "We hope someday to build an archway over the road to proclaim our parallel-ness, but for now we just have a bench and a small monument on the side of the road.

Keizer is just north of Salem; the 45th parallel monument is on River Road North, between the bank at 5140 and the fast food restaurant at 5130. For more information contact the Keizer Chamber of Commerce at (503) 393-9111 or visit www.keizerchamber.com.

Tallest Glockenspiel
Mt. Angel

Founded in 1867 by German pioneers, the town of Mt. Angel works hard to stay true to its Old World roots. Most all downtown store-fronts have a Bavarian theme, and each fall, during Oktoberfest, the streets erupt with German dancing, yodeling, and nonstop oompah music as more than 300,000 visitors feast on German wines, beers, and sausage; dance Bavarian folk dances; and cheer for their favorites in the wiener dog races.

Not content with their place in the record books as the home of Oregon's largest annual folk festival, the folks in Mt. Angel joined forces to construct the country's tallest glockenspiel. This 49-foot-tall tower has chromatically tuned bells, animated singing figures, and a giant clock. (Previously the tallest glockenspiel in the United States

Mustached-mascot: Pappa Oom Pah is a mustached mascot.
Mt. Angel Oktoberfest

★ ★

was the 45-foot tower in New Ulm, Minnesota, a town that also has German roots.)

Unveiled at the 2006 Oktoberfest, Mt. Angel's glockenspiel has action on several levels. The first floor has seven life-size, hand-carved wooden figures. Each figure represents a person or event in local history, and each rotates and turns to music. On the second floor, shutters open to reveal a boy and girl dressed in traditional Bavarian peasant costumes. This duo swings on a garden swing and sings the song "Edelweiss."

The glockenspiel is part of Mt. Angel's downtown Edelweiss building, which was built to resemble a large chalet with Alpine features such as balconies, pitched and gabled roofs, and lots of stucco. The building's upper floors provide affordable apartments for seniors who, you can imagine, might become less than enchanted with the hourly glockenspiel activity going on outside their windows. Never fear, say town officials: The building has great soundproofing, and the glockenspiel's last performance is at 7 p.m. each day.

Except, that is, during Oktoberfest, when performances continue until 11 p.m.

Mt. Angel's Oktoberfest is held each year beginning on the second Thursday after Labor Day and continuing through the following Sunday. The town is located about 18 miles northeast of Salem, on OR 214. For more information call (503) 845-9440 or go to www.oktoberfest.org.

World's Largest Hairball

Mt. Angel

The grounds of the century-old Benedictine monastery at the Mt. Angel Abbey and Seminary offer great views of the Willamette Valley and the Cascade foothills. Over in the library, designed by noted Finnish architect Alvar Aalto, display cases offer a glimpse into the monastery's extensive rare book collection. But for views of a quite different nature, make a beeline for the "collectobelia" (as one monk calls it) at the Mt. Angel Abbey Museum.

★ ★

On display in the "collectobelia," the
world's largest hairball—and friends.
Ross Reynolds

In the past rare religious artifacts and finely crafted souvenirs from
around the world were charmingly jumbled up in this basement
museum with a menagerie of taxidermied animals that includes a
polar bear, a bison, and a huge moose, as well as collections of eggs,
ships in bottles, and doorknobs. These days displays are more orderly,
with the religious garments and crown of thorns separated from the
paperweights, fossils, and South African beadwork.

What makes this museum a favorite among curiosity seekers, though, are the taxidermied calves—there's one here with eight legs and another with six legs—and what may just very well be the world's largest hairball.

According to the monks, the calf was born over in Tillamook in 1932 and was stuffed and brought to the museum because "they knew we would keep it." The hairballs, no doubt, were brought to the monks for similar reasons. While stored for years in a cardboard box, these days, five smooth, round hairballs from five different cows are carefully displayed alongside a hairy two-and-a-half-pound behemoth removed from the belly of a 300-pound hog in a meat-packing plant on September 19, 1941. At the time, the meat inspector on duty declared it to be the largest hairball he'd ever seen. Today the monks say the giant hairball is just "an example of God's creation."

Amen. Sort of makes you want to order the vegetable platter for lunch, doesn't it?

The hairballs and the taxidermied eight-legged calf are on display in the Mount Angel Abbey Museum. Admission is collected on the honor system; there's a box by the door. To reach the Mount Angel Abbey from I-5, take the Woodburn-Silverton exit and drive through Woodburn on OR 214 to Mt. Angel, then follow the signs to the abbey. For more information call (503) 845-3030 or visit www.mount angelabbey.org.

The Man Who Saved Christmas

Salem

Salem native A. C. Gilbert was a world-class athlete and one of the world's greatest and most prolific toy inventors. He won a gold medal for pole vaulting at the 1909 Olympics, earned a doctorate in medicine at Yale University, and received more than 150 patents for his inventions. Beginning in 1909, though, his toy company began winning the hearts of American children with American Flyer trains, Mysto Magic Sets, microscopes, chemistry sets, glassblowing kits, and

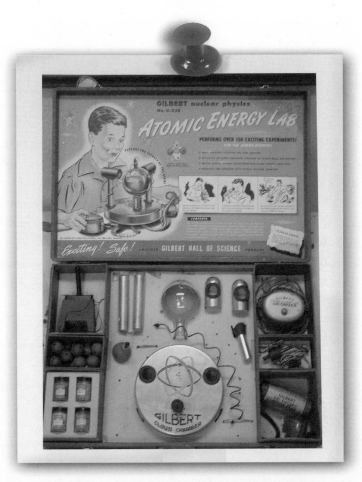

This atomic energy lab came complete
with radioactive source samples.
A. C. Gilbert's Discovery Village

Erector Sets—construction kits that could be used to build everything
from miniature working Ferris wheels to bridges using tiny metal
beams, nuts, screws, pulleys, gears, and electric motors.

But by far Gilbert's most unusual "toy" was the Atomic Energy
Lab. Sold from 1950 to 1951, the lab came with three radioactive
source samples, a Geiger counter, and a cloud chamber for splitting atoms. Included was an offer from the U.S. Government of up

to $10,000 for information on the whereabouts of large deposits of uranium.

Long before Gilbert's company sent boys and girls out in search of neighborhood uranium, Gilbert had already assured his place on the toy lovers' honor roll. During World War I, when Congress tried to turn Gilbert's toy factory into a munitions plant, the inventor went on the offensive. Armed with telescopes, microscopes, and other toys, Gilbert appeared before Congress and explained how, without toys to play with, the country would surely "lose a generation of doctors, engineers, and scientists." The plea worked: Gilbert's factory was allowed to stay open, and he became known as "the man who saved Christmas" for boys and girls everywhere.

Today a visit to A. C. Gilbert's Discovery Village is much like waking up on a toy-filled Christmas morning. In a series of historic houses and a huge outdoor discovery center, kids can immerse themselves in body-encompassing bubbles, pump up a pair of real human lungs, play on the world's largest outdoor Erector Set tower, explore a forest, and create their own toys in a room filled with vintage toys and inventions, including a working American Flyer model railroad, Gilbert puzzles, and rare Erector Sets.

A. C. Gilbert's Discovery Village is located at 116 Marion Street NE, under the Marion Street Bridge in Salem's Riverfront Park near the bank of the Willamette River. For more information call (503) 371-3631 or visit www.acgilbert.org.

Littlest Redwood Park
Salem

Back in 1872 Salem had plenty of trees. But yet a smooth-talking tree salesman from California was able to sell a Sierra redwood (*Sequoia giganta*) sapling to Judge William Waldo. The judge planted the tree on his property outside of town, but as the city grew, the judge's property—and the tree—ended up in the path of a major road.

Luckily the judge had connections. He had to give up his land but the tree was spared. In 1936 the Salem City Council declared the tree and the ground underneath it to be an official Salem city park. For a while the 12-by-20-foot plot of land known as Waldo Park was the World's Smallest Park.

Over the years the streets around Waldo Park have been widened and paved and have become increasingly congested. Proposals have been made to chop down what has been called a traffic hazard, but the judge's tree has persevered. And grown. Today the tree is more than 82 feet tall and has a trunk measuring 6 feet in diameter. It's so large that the main arterial that runs by it, Summer Street, has been squeezed from four lanes down to three lanes in order to make room for the tree.

And while at about 2 by 2 feet, Portland's Mill Ends Park is now credited as being the World's Smallest Park, Salem officials are proud that Waldo Park is now the World's Smallest Redwood Park.

Waldo Park is located at 605 Summer Street NE, on the northwest corner of the intersection of Union and Summer Streets in downtown Salem. If you bring a picnic, be prepared to eat it standing up.

Run, Rufus, Run
Salem

The Oregon State Fair has run for a few weeks each summer in Salem since about 1860. People come from far and wide to see and display prize vegetables and baked goods, handmade arts and crafts items, and animals large and small. But on opening day in 1979, a steer named Rufus ran away from the fair. And, it seems, with fairgoers' hearts.

An all-points bulletin was issued for the 1,000-pound steer, but despite being pursued by sheriff's ground units and helicopters, Rufus managed to elude capture by crossing the railroad tracks and swimming across the Willamette River. Sightings were reported, but every time the steer's owner, seventeen-year-old Scott Bernards, followed up on a lead, he'd arrive in a field to find that Rufus had moved on.

★ ★

For a while Bernards, a member of the Future Farmers of America, was worried that an unscrupulous farmer might have corralled Rufus and butchered him on the sly. But, luckily, after four weeks on the lam, Rufus was cornered and captured while he was munching on corn in a field 15 miles away from the fairgrounds.

Impressed by his moxie, fair officials purchased Rufus and, until his death in 1987, he was the fair's mascot and among its most popular attractions (although he was kept behind a secure double fence). When the fair wasn't in session, Rufus lived at the farm annex of the Oregon State Penitentiary in Salem and was cared for by prisoners, who no doubt also admired his moxie and his ability to elude the authorities.

Got Milk?

Salem

Rufus wasn't the first bovine to win the hearts of Oregonians visiting the Oregon State Fair. In the early 1900s there was Vive La France No. 319616 or, as she was better known, the Wonder Cow.

The milk from this champion cow was extraordinarily rich in butter fat, and at one time she held three world records. When she died, No. 319616 was buried at the Oregon State Fairgrounds in Salem, between the poultry building and the livestock pavilion.

We raise our (milk) glasses to you, Vive La France No. 319616.

Now, people don't just drink milk during a state fair, of course. During the eleven-day event, the fair becomes Oregon's second-largest city, with a hungry "population" of about 333,000. And according to fair officials, those folks eat an estimated 23,500 ears of roasted corn, 34,000 onions, 20,000 pounds of yakisoba noodles, and 27,500 potatoes that are made into 38,250 servings of curly fries and covered by 74,000 ounces of ketchup. In addition, the equivalent of 21,800 pounds of ground beef—or 65,400 burgers—are also consumed each year at the fair.

Maybe it was the hamburger count that sent Rufus running away from the fair.

★ ★

VIVE LA FRANCE NO. 319616
THE WONDER COW
HELD 3 WORLD RECORDS
AT ONE TIME.
PRODUCED IN 6 YEARS
TEST 5332 LBS. FAT
GRAND CHAMPION P.I.
PORTLAND ORE. 1919

PICKARD BROS. MARION ORE.

Every champion needs a good headstone.
Salem Convention & Visitors Bureau

The Oregon State Fair has been held in Salem at the end of the summer annually for more than 140 years. For more information call (503) 947-3247 or go to www.oregonstatefair.org.

Dog-gone Amazing
Silverton

In the summer of 1923, Frank and Elizabeth Brazier took their dog, Bobbie, with them when they went on a road trip back east from their home in Silverton. A mixture of shepherd and Scotch collie, Bobbie seemed perfectly happy riding on the running board or on top of the luggage. But somehow, once they all got to Indiana, Bobbie got

★ ★

Folks still marvel over the story of Bobbie the Wonder Dog.
Ross Reynolds

lost. The Braziers searched for him during their three-week visit but ended up going home, heartbroken, without him.

To everyone's shock and amazement, six months later—on February 15, 1924, to be exact—Bobbie showed up back home in Silverton. He was worn out, skinny, shaggy, and matted, but he was definitely Bobbie and, somehow, he'd found his way home. A newspaper account of the miraculous 3,000-mile trek chalked it up to Bobbie's "remarkable instinct or reasoning power," canine loyalty, or perhaps the draw of the Oregon climate.

Bobbie's amazing journey was featured in *Ripley's Believe It or Not!* and he was the star of the movie *Bobbie the Wonder Dog.* A book was written about the plucky pooch, and he was awarded a silver medal by the Oregon Humane Society. And three years later, when Bobbie died, more than 200 people—and fellow film star Rin Tin Tin—attended the funeral.

Today Bobbie's amazing feat is remembered each February 15 on Silverton's Bobbie Day and each May during the town's annual Pet Parade. Bobbie's memory is honored year-round as well: There's a mural by Laurie Webb depicting Bobbie's story, a concrete statue of Bobbie, and a replica of a special dog house he received in 1924.

The mural, statue, dog house, and an information board about Bobbie are located near downtown Silverton at the intersection of Water Street (OR 214) and Lewis Street. For more information call the Silverton Area Chamber of Commerce at (503) 873-5615 or visit www.silvertonchamber.org.

Couch Contest

Silverton

Once a year Silverton's Main Street is closed to cars but open to couches. It's not a citywide clean-up campaign but the Silvy 250, a series of wacky 250-foot timed races that pit steerable davenports and love seats against recliners and other tricked-out living room furniture. The rules are as simple as a straight-back chair: Upholstery may be pushed, pulled, or carried, but no electricity is allowed. "I love seeing how people dress up their couches," says Stacey Palmer, manager of the Silverton Area Chamber of Commerce, "but I'm always holding my breath because you never know if the furniture will stop once it gets rolling."

Careening couches on Main Street would draw crowds in any town, but Silverton's davenport races have a special meaning. They're part of a festival honoring Homer Davenport, the local boy who grew up to be an internationally known and highly paid political cartoonist for the Hearst newspaper syndicate in the late 1800s and early 1900s.

Davenport's popular, detailed pen-and-ink caricatures lampooned corporate behemoths and political bosses while championing the

★ ★

Don't delay the davenport.
Silverton Area Chamber of Commerce

average man. The influential cartoonist wrote books and lectured, but he also had a passion for horses. In 1906 Davenport traveled to the Bedouin Desert and brought back twenty-seven pure-blooded Arabian horses. To this day horses descended from those initial imports are called Davenport Arabians.

Unfortunately, Davenport died of pneumonia at age forty-five, just three days after penning an illustration about the sinking of the *Titanic*. But every year, on the first full weekend in August, Silverton celebrates Homer Davenport Days with couch races on Main Street and food, music, and the annual Homer Davenport International Cartoon Contest in nearby Coolidge-McClaine Park.

Silverton is about 44 miles south of Portland on OR 214. For more information on Davenport Days, contact the Silverton Area Chamber of Commerce at (503) 873-5615 or visit www.davenportdays.com.

Benefit for Bacteria

Springfield

Sometimes small things bring people together. Like the live bacteria that brought the Grateful Dead to the rescue of a small Oregon creamery.

In 1960 Chuck and Sue Kesey spun off a small business from the family's creamery. Chuck, the brother of author Ken Kesey (author of *One Flew Over the Cuckoo's Nest* and *Sometimes a Great Notion*), along with his wife, Sue, began by supplying returnable gallon glass jugs of milk to other area creameries. It was at the beginning of the counterculture and natural foods movement, so the couple also tried their hand at making yogurt.

At the urging of their bookkeeper, Nancy, the Keseys used live cultures in the yogurt, and soon the company became the first creamery in the United States to sell acidophilus-cultured yogurt. The tangy treat became a staple at local co-ops and health food stores, and after getting a call from a store asking for more of "that Nancy's yogurt," the Keseys decided to name the whole brand in her honor. At first the product was only available locally, but sales got a boost when two young entrepreneurs in the Bay Area, including now–music legend Huey Lewis, added Nancy's Yogurt to their underground comic book route and let it be known that Nancy's Yogurt had a connection to Ken Kesey.

The connection to the notorious counterculture legend paid off in 1972, when the creamery company hit hard times. Chuck Kesey asked the Grateful Dead to come to Eugene from California and play a benefit concert for the creamery. Tickets were printed on the Nancy's Yogurt containers, and more than 20,000 people attended. A movie of that first concert, titled *Sunshine Daydream*, was made, and the Kesey family went on to sponsor at least a dozen other Grateful Dead concerts in the Eugene area during the 1980s and early 1990s.

Trash or Treasure?

Springfield

Once known for its flour and lumber mills, this city is so proud of its past that the downtown is dotted with more than twenty historic murals, and the 1911 Oregon Power Company transformer station across from City Hall has been turned into a museum. Wander through town guided by the walking tour brochure handed out by

Thousands of items retrieved from the sewers ended up in this city seal.

the Visitor Information Center, but be sure to leave time to visit City Hall.

Outside the building there's an unusual sculpture titled *The Balancing Act* that features a rhinoceros balancing a gymnast who is holding a bird of prey. Don't spend too much time pondering the sculpture's meaning; the real treat is indoors. There you'll find a huge mosaic replica of the city's seal made entirely of items dredged from Springfield's first-ever sewer cleaning.

This unusual piece of folk art was created in 1972 by artist and former city employee Russell Ziolkowski. He salvaged thousands of items when he helped jet clean the city's sanitary sewer system. More than 4,200 items found their way into his seventy-pound version of the city seal.

Now encased in a clear, resin-like material and locked in a special vitrine, the seal offers up many treasures: Look closely and you'll see a gold nugget, charms, shells, a diamond pin, a tiny revolver, false teeth, a jackknife, a French perfume bottle, coins, clay marbles, bullets, and a dog tag from 1942.

Springfield is located just east of I-5, near Eugene. The Visitor Information Center is in the Springfield Depot at Pioneer Parkway West and South A Street. City Hall is at 225 Fifth Street. For more information call the Springfield Chamber of Commerce at (866) 346-1651 or go to www.springfield-chamber.org.

Over Easy
Sublimity

Al Faussett was a Northwest logger-turned-daredevil who gained notoriety by strapping himself into homemade canoes and throwing himself over waterfalls. Along the way he broke ribs, wrists, and records.

He did it first in May 1926, when he went over 104-foot Sunset Falls on the Skykomish River in Washington State in a homemade 34-foot spruce canoe. That day 3,000 people paid $1 each just to watch—and Faussett was hooked.

He later tackled the treacherous waters of Spokane Falls on the Spokane River in Washington, Shoshone Falls on the Snake River in Idaho, Celilo Falls on the Columbia River, and, with more than 10,000 people watching, Oregon City Falls on the Willamette River near Portland.

In 1928 5,000 onlookers were on hand when Faussett attempted to ride down the 177-foot South Falls on Silver Creek near Sublimity, which is now part of Silver Falls State Park. For this stunt he built a 180-pound orange canvas–covered boat and stuffed it with thirty-six inner tubes. And while he survived the fall, he broke several ribs and one wrist, sprained both his ankles, and spent six weeks in the local hospital.

Faussett's ultimate goal was to run Niagara Falls, even though he'd conquered Shoshone Falls, which is 45 feet higher. He never got around to making that trip, but for years, usually on the weekend after July fourth, folks have been gathering at Silver Falls State Park to celebrate Al Faussett Days with games, a pie social, and exhibits demonstrating how people lived during the Great Depression.

There's usually a canoe race as well, with small, numbered, canoe-shaped blocks of wood sent over the falls to a pool below, and prizes for the owners of the first "boats" to cross the finish line. No one, however, is allowed to try to reenact Faussett's feat. "I always wonder why we celebrate a stunt we wouldn't let anyone attempt now," says one park staffer, "but it's still a lot of fun." Especially because members of the Faussett family usually show up to share stories of their daring relative and to show a video of the dramatic newsreel documenting his South Falls plunge.

Silver Falls State Park is located about 26 miles east of Salem, between Silverton and Sublimity. The park's Canyon Trail leads past ten waterfalls, ranging from 27-foot Drake Falls to 177-foot South Falls. From OR 22 take OR 214 to the park. The Al Faussett Days celebration was on hiatus for a year or two, so be sure to call ahead if you're planning on showing up. For more information call (503) 873-8681 or visit www.oregonstateparks.org/park_211.php.

Found Underground
Sweet Home

In 1950 Ken White was using a Geiger counter to search for uranium to sell to the U.S. Government for use in atomic bombs and reactors. The machine required the user to wear headphones, so White wasn't able to hear the rattlesnake he was about to step on until it was almost too late. That close call led him to invent and manufacture a Geiger counter, and later a series of metal detectors, that had speakers instead of headphones. White became known as the Henry Ford of the metal detector industry, and today the company he founded is one of the largest in the field. His son and his wife now run the business.

This barnacle-encrusted pistol was still loaded when it was pulled from the sea.
Melissa Wise

★ ★

Many of us are familiar with the use of metal detectors by amateur and professional treasure hunters. But the folks at White's Electronics say the machines are also used in police and FBI investigations and are often installed at bakeries and packing plants to detect nuts and bolts that may fall into the food products. Some hospitals even use metal detectors to make sure that no surgical instruments are left behind in patients after operations.

Over the years White's manufacturing plant in Sweet Home has accumulated quite a collection of items discovered with their metal detectors, so they've set aside one room at the factory as a museum. Step inside to see Geiger counters dating back to the 1950s (including the model White was using when he encountered that rattlesnake), unearthed cash boxes, Civil War–era bullets and cannon balls, a sword, old coins, and a barnacle-encrusted pistol that the late Ken White recovered while treasure-diving on the wreck site of a Spanish fleet that sunk in the 1700s off the Florida coast. Although it was completely encrusted in coral, X-rays revealed that the pistol was still loaded.

White's Electronics Museum is free and open to the public. It's located at the headquarters of White's Electronics at 1101 Pleasant Valley Road in Sweet Home. From US 20 in Sweet Home, turn onto Pleasant Valley Road (there's a feed store and a car lot on the corner) and take the first left after the bridge. White's Electronics is at the end of that road. The museum is next to the main office and demonstration room. For more information call (541) 367-6121 or go to www.whiteselectronics.com.

5

Southern Oregon

We've tucked the curiosities on the southern coast into the Oregon Coast chapter, so here we've listed discoveries that lie south of Cottage Grove along the I-5 corridor down toward the California border plus spots found east of the Siskiyou Mountains and over in Lake County. Highlights here include town "mascots" that range from rowdy cavemen and pistol-toting cowboys to giant mosquitoes and Paul Bunyan's little brother, Ralph.

In Ashland you can learn why a dip in the rotten-egg-smelling, lithium-laced water is supposed to do wonders for ailing bodies. In Cave Junction you can join a guided tour of the Oregon Caves and study cave curiosities that include cave popcorn, cave kisses, and moon milk. And in Gold Hill you can (some say must!) visit the Oregon Vortex, a whirlpool of weirdness that has been entertaining, mystifying, and inclining visitors towards magnetic north since the 1930s.

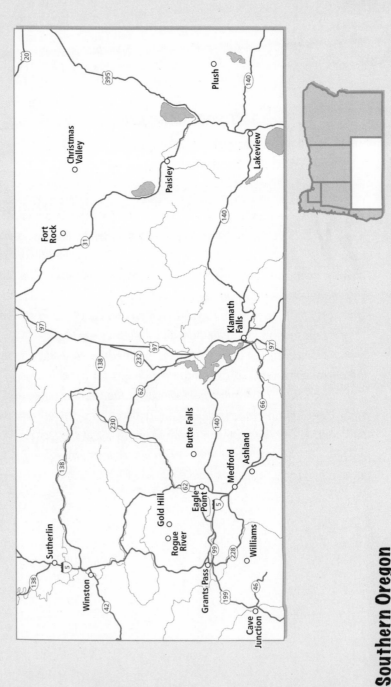

Southern Oregon

Saratoga of the West

Ashland

Ashland is best known these days as the home of the Oregon Shakespeare Festival, the largest classic repertory theater in the country. More than 350,000 theater lovers trek here each year to gorge on Shakespeare productions and contemporary theater offerings. But once, folks came here simply to sip the water.

Not just any water, but the naturally-carbonated, lithium-laced water discovered in 1907 flowing from a spring near town. Called Lithia Water due to a lithium level second only to New York's famous Saratoga Springs, Ashland was dubbed the Saratoga of the West. Thought to have healing powers, the rotten-egg-flavored, mineral-rich water was highly sought out; people bathed in it, drank it, and cooked with it.

Folks have been drinking the Lithia-laced water for years.
Chester Stevens; Terry Skibby collection

★ ★

Loaded with sulfur, sodium, calcium, and chlorine in addition to lithium, Lithia Water became so popular that in 1914 the citizens of Ashland passed a bond to purchase the Lithia Springs property and pipe the potion to town. For years Lithia Water flowed freely at the downtown Lithia Park, at the railroad station, at the Carnegie Library, and at several hotels around town. Today Lithia Water is still available from a restored fountain at the Plaza on Main Street in downtown Ashland, which sits on the edge of ninety-three-acre Lithia Park, a lovely spot now recognized as a National Historic Site.

If you should find yourself parched near downtown Ashland, be forewarned. There are actually two public fountains on the Plaza; one dispenses "regular" water while the other teems with somewhat foul-tasting Lithia Water. A favorite pastime of locals is to point out-of-towners to the Lithia Water fountain and laugh uproariously when someone gulps down the yucky-tasting brew.

It's the Water
Ashland

If the idea of bathing in water that some say can heal everything from depression to poison ivy sounds appealing, consider a night at the Lithia Springs Resort. It claims to be the only Ashland-area hotel that pipes the warm mineral water directly into the rooms from a source underground.

The resort's general manager says that although the mineral content does make the water smell a bit sulfury no one really seems to mind. "The water is why folks come here. That's what comes out of the sinks in the guest rooms. Bathing in it, especially in our two-person tubs, is very soothing." And while they're not allowed to make any formal claims about the water, people do believe that it has "medicinal advantages" and so they also use Lithia Water in the treatments at the on-site Waterstone Spa and in its mineral tubs and steam rooms.

Some say the Lithia waters have "medicinal advantages."
Opi Snow

For a less formal encounter with Lithia Water, head next door to the very laid-back Jackson Wellsprings. This RV park and tent campground pipes the warm mineral water into a large swimming pool, a hydrotherapy pool, and a series of private soaking tubs.

The Lithia Springs Resort and Waterstone Spa are located at 2165 West Jackson Road, about 3 miles from downtown Ashland. For more information call (800) 482-7128 or visit www.ashlandinn.com. Jackson Wellsprings is located nearby, at 2253 OR 99 N. For more information about Jackson Wellsprings Hot Springs Spa and Campground, call (541) 482-3776 or go to www.jacksonwellsprings.com.

★ ★

CSI Bambi
Ashland

If a bear is illegally shot in the woods, who you gonna call?

Probably the scientists at the world's only crime lab dedicated entirely to wildlife. Founded in 1975, the Ashland-based National Fish and Wildlife Forensics Laboratory is part of the U.S. Fish and Wildlife Service and a key partner in close to a thousand cases a year.

Like "regular" police crime labs, the job of investigators at the wildlife crime lab is to identify and compare evidence that can show a link between a suspect, a victim, and a crime scene. The difference here: All the victims are wild animals. And so, according to lab director Ken Goddard, that means his staff of thirty-six studies everything from blood and tissue samples to hides, furs, talons, tusks, claws,

Ashland is home to a crime lab for critters.
National Fish & Wildlife Forensics Lab

stomach contents, and anything else that may have come from—or been inside—an animal. Objects made from animals—including reptile-skin purses, boots, and shoes; carved ivory; and "medicinals" such as rhino horn pills and tiger bone juice—are also studied.

Goddard says his team tries to steer clear of the tabloid cases concerning the occasional spate of cow mutilations involving, for example, drained blood and slit eyelids, that some believe is linked to cults, secret government projects, or aliens sent to Earth to bring back cow parts. "That's more of a property crime," explains Goddard. But he says once in a while his lab will examine a bit of Bigfoot evidence from the field. "Usually it's a bit of hair that a wildlife officer has found. So far it's always turned out to be polyester."

Because the lab is so busy, and because they work with toxins, poisons, and potentially diseased carcasses, the Wildlife Forensics Lab isn't open for tours. But you may be able to get a whiff of what goes on here by reading one of the novels Ken Goddard pens in his off-duty time about "professional terrorists, underground chemists, demented burglars, and malicious poachers."

To find out more about the National Fish and Wildlife Forensics Laboratory, go to www.lab.fws.gov.

Close the Gate behind You
Butte Falls

The former logging town of Butte Falls is located about 40 miles northeast of Medford. While tiny—the population is around 440 people—the town has its own waterfall, two historical museums, two restaurants, and a general store.

Butte Falls is also the only town to be entirely surrounded by a barbed wire fence. While locals sometimes joke that the barrier was put there to keep residents from leaving, it's clear from the two cattle guards at either end of town that the fence actually helps keep livestock out on the range.

Paul Bunyan's little brother is always on duty.
Cory Hamann

✦ ✦

Don't let the fence keep you out. Visitors—human or bovine—
who do make it into town are welcomed by an unusual sight. Standing on a 3-foot stump in City Park is a 6-foot statue of Ralph Bunyan,
the not-so-well-known or talked-about younger brother of mythic
lumberjack Paul Bunyan. Carved by noted local logger and folk artist
Bill Edmondson, the statue is now cared for by Karen Davis, a logger
and longtime town resident who says Edmondson carved the statue
at the request of local citizens who wanted "something special to
stand guard over the town's tiny park."

To find Butte Falls, turn right off OR 62, 4.5 miles north of Eagle
Point, and take the Butte Falls Highway approximately 25 miles to town.

Cave Kisses
Cave Junction

On a hunting expedition in the Siskiyou Mountains back in 1874,
Elijah Davidson ended up chasing after his dog, Bruno, who was
chasing after a bear, whose name is not known. The bear led Bruno
and Davidson into a hole in a mountainside that led to a dark and
mysterious cave. Davidson and his dog got lost in the cave and the
bear got away, but they ended up discovering an incredibly magical spot. Explorers who returned to the cave found a network of 3
miles of underground caverns, complete with a fast-running stream
dubbed the River Styx. Inside the caverns were narrow passageways
and beautiful marble formations, fanciful stalactites and stalagmites,
and an amazing array of natural cave sculptures.

In 1907 Joaquin Miller, the "poet of the Sierras," visited the
cave and eloquently described what he called the "Marble Halls of
Oregon." That drew the attention of folks in Washington, D.C., and
in 1909 President William Taft set aside 480 acres around the cave
as the Oregon Caves National Monument. Today tour guides from
the National Park Service lead visitors on ninety-minute walking tours
of the cave, past rock formations that resemble giant ghosts, billowy
parachutes, huge whale ribs, and a sea of underground waves. Along

★ ★

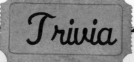

Cave Curiosities

- The Oregon Caves system appears to have developed in rocks that were once an ancient, Jurassic-era, tropical ocean reef.

- The caves are home to bats, moths, crickets, snails, slugs, spiders, and a community of cave-adapted insects including the grylloblattid, a relic of the ice age.

- There are four hiking trails at the Oregon Caves National Monument. One of them, the Big Tree Trail, takes hikers past the largest Douglas fir known to exist in Oregon.

- The Chateau is a rustic six-story hotel established in 1934 at the Oregon Caves National Monument. When it's open for lodging (late April through October), day visitors are welcome to stop in to see the huge, marble, double fireplace in the fourth-floor lobby and to have dinner at the fine-dining room or, better yet, lunch in the 1930s-style coffee shop and soda fountain downstairs.

the way visitors are introduced to cave popcorn, cave kisses (drips of water), and moon milk, a cottage cheese–like substance created by calcite crystals that's also known as "gnome milk," a wound-healing folk medicine left as a gift by elves who lived in the cave.

The elves may have moved on, but the caves are constantly being explored and restored, and new discoveries are being made all the time. For instance, a grizzly bear bone discovered in the cave not long ago may be the oldest grizzly fossil ever found in North America. And jaguar bones found in the cave that are somewhere between 12,000 to 20,000 years old are, to date, the northernmost jaguar remains discovered anywhere in the world.

★ ★

The Oregon Caves National Monument is 30 miles southwest of Grants Pass. Tours of the caves are offered year-round (except Thanksgiving and Christmas). To reach the caves, take US 199 to Cave Junction and travel 20 miles east on OR 46 to the park entrance. (Note: The last 8 miles of this trip are on narrow, windy roads not recommended for trailers.) For more information call the Oregon Caves National Monument at (541) 592-2100 or visit www.nps.gov/orca.

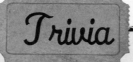

Oregon Caves Food Formations

Following is a guide to "food formations" in the Oregon Caves, as explained by Roger Brandt from the National Park Service.

- Gnome milk is also known as moon milk (*mondmilch*), a type of cave formation created by bacteria growth. The bacteria (*actinomycete*) that create these formations are the same as the one used to make a variety of antibiotics, including Neosporin and streptomycin.

- Cave popcorn is a formation created by evaporation. It typically grows where natural winds in the cave blow against its walls so you might find it on one side of a rock and not the other. The popcorn points into the wind, which often blows into the cave through an opening to the outside. If you were lost in a cave, you could follow the popcorn to the nearest opening. This is why these rocks are also called "compass stones."

- Cave bacon is a formation created by drops of water that flow down the sides of the cave. Some people claim that the different-colored banding in cave bacon is a record of ancient climate change.

B&B in the Trees

Cave Junction

Many of us have spent a vacation night in a posh hotel, at a road-side motel, in a tent at a campground, or on the couch at a friend's house. But the folks at the Out 'n' About Treesort have another over-night option: a comfortable, full-size bed in a tree house.

Encouraging guests to "go out on a limb," Michael Garnier and his friends have built eighteen different tree houses suitable for

Treehouses go upscale at the Treesort.
Out 'n' About Treesort

overnight stays at their thirty-six-acre "treesort"—as in resort—in southern Oregon. These are not your rickety, nailed-together, gathered-up-scrapwood types of tree houses, but sturdy, lovingly built cabins—really—that just happen to be sitting up in the trees.

The Tree Room Schoolhouse Suite, for example, sleeps four and has a kitchen, a bathroom, and a dining area. The Swiss Family Complex is actually a pair of tree houses connected by a swinging bridge. And the Cavaltree is a two-story tree house with an observation deck and swinging bridge that leads to the Treeloon, a tree house inspired by old Wild West saloons.

Ironically, for many years the Treesort had to operate as an underground, word-of-mouth operation because building permits for tree houses could not be secured. But after much legal wrangling, the Treesort became a licensed bed-and-breakfast establishment.

These days activities at the Out 'n' About Treesort have branched out to include music events and the Treehouse Institute, which offers workshops in climbing and tree house construction, a summer camp for families, and tours of the facility for folks who aren't quite convinced it's possible to have a pleasant, knotty night sleeping in the trees. And each October the Treesort hosts the annual World Treehouse Association Conference, which includes lectures on choosing trees for tree houses and the ins and outs of rigging, layout, and design.

The Treesort is located south of Cave Junction at 300 Page Creek Road. For more information call (541) 592-2208 or go to www.tree houses.com.

Letter-Writing Tips
Christmas Valley

There are about one hundred towns and cities in the United States with holiday-related names, and the post offices in most of them will re-mail your holiday cards for you after adding a local postmark. That way your favorite niece or nephew can be impressed and amazed when they open the mailbox and see a Christmas card postmarked from North Pole, Alaska, or from Rudolph, Wisconsin.

Unusual postmarks are fun, but at least a dozen towns really get into the holiday spirit with specially designed festive cancellations. Oregon's Christmas Valley post office is one of them. Darrell Krabill serves as postmaster at the contract post office here, and he's the Santa's helper who stamps the "spur-on-the-ice-skate" cancellation on more than 1,000 letters each year. "It's fun to see where all the cards come from," he says, "and sometimes people send me a special holiday card and, once in a blue moon, I've even gotten a gift."

If you'd like your holiday cards to bear the special Christmas Valley cancellation stamp, here's what to do: Address, seal, and put postage stamps on the envelopes you want to be mailed. Put them all together in a larger envelope and send them to the attention of Christmas Re-Mailing, Christmas Valley, OR 97641.

Holiday cards get special attention at the Christmas Valley Post Office.
Christmas Valley Post Office

If you want to make sure that your cards arrive in time for Christmas, you should get your package to the post office by December 15. The earlier the better: Much like post offices everywhere, the Christmas Valley one gets very busy during the holiday season, and Postmaster Krabill is usually the only elf on duty.

Hollywood Moos
Eagle Point

Although she was known worldwide as Fred Astaire's glamorous on-screen dancing partner and love interest, from the 1940s until 1990 the folks around Eagle Point thought of actress Ginger Rogers as "the movie star with the cows."

Around 1940 Rogers bought a 1,000-acre ranch on the Rogue River near Eagle Point. She built a dairy on the farm and bred Guernsey cows that provided some of the milk to nearby Camp White, which hosted almost 25,000 soldiers during World War II. In addition to running the 4R (the Rogers Rogue River Ranch), the actress was known to enjoy fishing on the Rogue River each summer and playing hostess to other Hollywood stars seeking a vacation in the country.

But long before Rogers bought her ranch, she had a connection with southern Oregon. In 1925 she won a statewide Charleston dance competition in Texas. That led to a contract for a six-month theater tour of one-night performances, and on April 21, 1926, Rogers appeared onstage at a local theater, Hunt's Craterian, in Medford. The local newspaper took note. It printed a picture of the then-fifteen-year-old Rogers and gave this review: "Miss Rogers is a winsome little miss with captivating mannerisms and a pair of feet that make the most intricate dances seem easy."

Rogers returned to the theater in 1993 for a benefit event that included an interview and a screening of her movie *Roxy Hart*. Today the theater is named the Craterian Ginger Rogers Theater in her honor.

Ginger Rogers died in 1995 at the age of eighty-three, but the folks in Eagle Point still remember her—and her cows. The Eagle

Point Museum has a case filled with memorabilia associated with celebrities from the area that includes photos of Rogers and an assortment of milk bottles from her dairy. The museum is located in the historic district of Eagle Point, on North Royal Avenue. For more information call (541) 826-4166.

The Craterian Ginger Rogers Theater is located in Medford, 12 miles away, at 23 South Central Avenue. For more information call (541) 779-3000 or visit www.craterian.org.

Holes and Cracks in the Ground
Fort Rock

Oregon's Outback Scenic Highway runs from La Pine to the California border, through an isolated rural area near Fort Rock filled with a variety of geologic oddities including a place called Hole-in-the-Ground and one called Crack-in-the-Ground.

Hole-in-the-Ground is a huge, 300-foot "dip" in the ground that looks as if a meteor hit it, but scientists say that this mile-wide crater is actually the result of volcanic activity. However it got here, the spot is so out-of-this-world-looking that in 1966 astronauts were sent to the hole to experience what it might be like to be on the moon.

Outside Christmas Valley, not too far down the road from Hole-in-the-Ground, is a spot called Crack-in-the-Ground. This basalt lava fissure is about 2 miles long, 10 to 15 feet wide, and more than 70 feet deep. Cracks in the ground like this are usually the result of earthquakes or volcanic activity, and they're usually filled up with rocks or lava. But Crack-in-the-Ground is unusual in that it's stayed "empty" for more than 1,000 years now.

In the old days locals simply called this unusually cool spot "the Crack" and used it as a picnic area and as a source of ice for homemade ice cream. Today there's a hiking trail along the bottom of the fissure, where temperatures are often as much as twenty degrees cooler than up above.

✦ ✦

To reach the Hole-in-the-Ground, head south from Bend on US 97 to La Pine, then go southeast on OR 31 for about 22 miles and follow the signs to Hole-in-the-Ground (about 4 miles). To reach Crack-in-the-Ground, return to OR 31 and go east to Christmas Valley. "The Crack" is about 8 miles north of Christmas Valley on gravel BLM Road 61090; look for signs on the highway. For more information call the Christmas Valley Chamber of Commerce at (541) 576-3838 or visit www.christmas valley.org or www.fortrockmuseum.com/crack1.htm.

Whirlpool of Weirdness
Gold Hill

Since 1930 folks have been flocking to the Oregon Vortex to experience "the famous circular area with its unique phenomena."

Sound mysterious? It is. Sound corny? It's that, too. And that's why we love it.

Things are not what they seem at the Oregon Vortex.

★ ★

But what is it? That's hard to say. It's a mysterious plot of land, less than an acre, in southern Oregon where the documented laws of physics seem to be out of whack and where gravity goes giddy. Short people appear taller than they really are. Balls appear to roll uphill. And brooms seemingly stand upright on their own.

What makes all this strange stuff happen? That's hard to say as well. It may be a natural occurrence. Or not. Guides at the Vortex will tell you that the Native Americans who lived in the area long ago called this spot the Forbidden Ground and stayed clear. Birds and other wildlife supposedly avoided the area as well.

But none of that strange stuff stopped the Grey Eagle Mining Company from building a gold assay office here in the 1890s. Known now as the House of Mystery, the assay office slid downhill in 1910 during a particularly rainy season. When it stopped sliding it was skewed up against a maple tree, where it still sits, like a drunk up against a light pole.

We'd like to say that visitors will be bowled over by the "whirl-pool of force" in effect here. But it's actually safer to predict, as the Vortex owners do, that "inevitably the visitor assumes a posture that inclines toward magnetic north."

The House of Mystery at the Oregon Vortex is located at 4303 Sardine Creek Road in Gold Hill, which is between Medford and Grants Pass. From I-5, take exit 43. The vortex is 4 miles off of OR 235. For more information call (877) 386-7839 or go to www.oregonvortex.com.

Beers for Bunyan
Grants Pass

Paul Bunyan sure does get around. People have written stories about him, told tall tales about him, and penned songs and sonnets about him. His image shows up in everything from postcards and picture books to stained-glass windows. And in Oregon, statues of the big guy appear in some surprising places, such as on top of the Cedar-wood Saloon in Grants Pass.

★ ★

Bar-Bunyan keeps watch over the Cedarwood Saloon.
Bruce Mesman

When Bruce and Tamerie Mesman bought the bar in 1991, there was already a 15-foot-tall statue set on top of the building. It wasn't Paul Bunyan, though. What they inherited was a muffler-man-type statue depicting a miner. He had blond hair, a pick ax, and a red shirt. Nearby was an authentic, rusty ore cart full of rocks spray-painted gold.

The Mesmans hadn't planned on giving the miner a major make-over, but they soon had no choice. A property-line dispute turned ugly, and a neighboring business owner hired a boom truck to take the miner down and drag him across the roadway to what was without a doubt saloon property. In the process the statue sustained wounds to his fiberglass torso and to his head, but after a three-week restoration and recuperation, he reappeared on top of the building, this time "reborn" as Paul Bunyan, with tidy brown hair, green shirt, an ax, denim-colored pants, and black boots.

Over the years the burly bar-Bunyan has proven to be as heroic as the mythic Bunyan we've all heard about. Mounted on a cement plat-form and secured to a pole that also advertises the Oregon lottery, the statue has survived vandalism attempts, car crashes, pellet gun attacks, and a windstorm that blew Bunyan's giant head right into his beefy arms.

The Mesmans say they don't know if the statue had to go through as many trials and tribulations when it was a miner, but now that he's Paul Bunyan and "we've all become quite fond of him," they'll make sure he survives.

You can visit this Paul Bunyan anytime. He's outside the Cedar-wood Saloon at 1345 Redwood Avenue in Grants Pass. For more information call (541) 479-6160.

Home of the Caveman
Grants Pass

At 18 feet tall, the muscular, primitive-looking guy in an animal-skin tunic standing on a rock pedestal at the north entrance of town is hard to miss.

This gruff-looking fiberglass caveman statue has been Grants Pass's Neanderthal-era mascot since 1971. However, the area's

★ ★

caveman connection dates back to 1922, when a group of local businessmen formed the Realm of Cavemen to promote tourism in the
area.

It's never too soon to look forward to retirement.
Monte Sanford, SAGA Design

For years, at just about any town event, Cavemen Club members could be counted on to show up clutching caveman clubs, drinking "saber-toothed tiger blood," and wearing horsehair wigs and bits of animal skins and furs. Rumors spread about club members eating raw meat during secret initiation rites. And during parades, rodeos, and festivals, costume-clad cavemen would reach into the crowds to "capture" onlookers, especially pretty women, and "lock" them up in stick and rawhide cages.

During its heyday the Cavemen Club was said to have more than 300 members, some of whom helped welcome celebrities, presidents, and presidential hopefuls passing through the area. Thomas Dewey was greeted in 1948, for example, and John F. and Jacqueline Kennedy were welcomed by cavemen at the regional airport in 1959. Shirley Temple, Babe Ruth, and Ronald Reagan also got the caveman treatment.

Unfortunately, membership in the Realm of Cavemen has dwindled over time, and there are just a few cavemen left in town. And on July 4, 2004, local vandals set fire to the caveman statue. For a while it looked as if the caveman was going to go the way of the dinosaurs, but Cavemen Club members rallied townspeople around their nifty Neanderthal and raised funds to repair the statue. To the delight of many, and the chagrin of some, the caveman was returned to his pedestal in 2005. Thanks to the handiwork of a local fiberglass expert, the town's mascot is now about 200 pounds heavier and made from a flame-retardant material that's almost indestructible.

Despite his refurbishment, the caveman's days may be numbered. These days Grants Pass boosters would like the town to be known for its recreational attractions and as the place "Where the Rogue River Runs," rather than the "Home of the Caveman." But it's hard to break with tradition, especially when the town is filled with caveman "things," including Caveman Pool, Caveman Bridge (now listed on the National Register of Historic Places), and Caveman High School, which is the home of the Cavemen and the Lady Cavers. There are also more than two dozen clubs and businesses with caveman references, including Caveman Travel, Caveman Bowl, Caveman Kiwanis, the Caveman Vintage Car Club, and Caveman Towing.

Grants Pass is on I-5, about 60 miles north of the California border. The caveman statue is at the north end of town at Sixth Street.

Downed Douglas
Klamath Falls

Like the old saying, "The bigger they are, the harder they fall," when the world's largest Douglas fir tree toppled over, the thud was felt statewide.

Seven-thousand-pound slices of this downed Douglas fir were exhibited around the state.
Oregon Parks and Recreation Department

★ ★

In 1962 folks in Oregon rejoiced when a 702-year-old, 200-foot-tall Douglas fir measuring 15.8 feet in diameter was officially designated the World's Largest Douglas Fir. But later that year, when a blustery sou'wester with hurricane-force winds blew down the coast, the stately behemoth crashed to the ground.

It was a sad day for tree lovers and a sad day for Crown-Zellerbach, the paper-manufacturing company on whose Seaside-area tree farm the champion Douglas fir had been growing. But in keeping with that other old saying, "When life give you lemons, make lemonade," the company decided that in the same way the ashes of a deceased loved one are sometimes distributed to various family members, 7,000-pound slices of the fallen Douglas fir would be presented to logging communities throughout the state.

A half-dozen communities got slices, and today a slice of that record-setting tree is just one of the hundreds of items on display at the sprawling Logging Museum in Collier Memorial State Park north of Klamath Falls. With more than twelve acres of open-air exhibits, the museum is considered to be the world's largest logging museum, with steam donkeys, log loaders, spar poles, chain saws, and other antique logging equipment reaching back to the mid-1800s.

It's sometimes hard to imagine some of these giant, rusting machines at work in the woods, so on Friday, Saturday, and Sunday evenings during the summer, campground park rangers offer interpretive programs with old-time logging movies. According to one ranger, "These aren't Hollywood movies that just happen to have scenes set in the woods. These are movies that show historical logging equipment in action." We've heard that Paul Bunyan shows up sometimes, with a giant tub of popcorn.

Collier Memorial State Park is located 30 miles north of Klamath Falls on US 97. The open-air Logging Museum is open year-round; the campground is usually open April through October. For more information call (541) 783-2471 or visit www.oregonstateparks.org/park_228.php.

✦ ✦

Warm and Toasty
Klamath Falls

Throughout history, hot water from underground geothermal reservoirs has been harnessed for a wide variety of uses. The Romans used it to treat eye and skin diseases. Native Americans used water from hot springs for cooking and medicine. And relaxing in warm pools fed by the "magic water" from natural hot springs is a popular activity worldwide.

Many towns and cities lucky enough to sit atop geothermal areas drill wells to access the natural resource, and they use the hot water and released steam to heat homes and businesses. In the Klamath Falls area, they've been doing this since the early 1900s, when the artesian flow from local hot springs was used to heat several homes.

In the 1930s a geothermal heating system was built into the local high school, and in the 1940s geothermal heat was used in a highway de-icing system. Today the city has one of the largest district heating systems in the United States. Originally created to serve just fourteen public buildings, the system now provides heat to many more commercial and public customers, including a greenhouse, a hospital, and more than 1,000 homes.

If you visit Klamath Falls during the winter, you'll notice that even during the iciest conditions, several downtown roads and sidewalks remain clear. That's because hot water runs through pipes installed underneath many parts of the downtown area, including the streets.

A Tall Tale
Lakeview

Like the folks in Lakeview, this lanky cowboy is tall and proud and seems glad to see ya when you drive into town. And why not? Lakeview serves as the Lake County seat. The Warner Mountains just east of town makes this area the self-proclaimed Hang Gliding Capital of the West. And, if you give them a chance, folks around here will be

Even cowboys need an occasional attitude adjustment.
Lake County Chamber of Commerce

sure to tell you that, at 4,800 feet above sea level, this town just 16 miles north of the California state line is the tallest town in Oregon.

The sweet, handsome cowboys stationed at the three entrances to town are replacements for the fellas that stood at these spots for years. The old cowboys were much taller, skinnier, and more somber-looking. And each had a pistol in his hand. Town boosters decided that the old cowboys weren't all that welcoming and arranged to put them out to pasture at the local fairgrounds at 1900 North Fourth Street. The new cowboys are on duty at OR 140 on the west side of town and on US 395 at the north and south sides.

Thar She Blows
Lakeview

The Tallest Town in Oregon has another claim to fame: It's the home of Old Perpetual. This geothermal natural wonder is the only active hot-water geyser in the Pacific Northwest, spouting a plume of 200-degree water over 60 feet in the air about every ninety seconds (except in the fall, when irrigation programs lower the water table and interrupt the geyser's schedule).

The 150-foot-diameter pool at the base of the geyser was once home to bluefish that adapted to life in hot water, but today it seems that only a few hearty goldfish swim there. In the 1920s the geyser (and two others which no longer exist) was also the centerpiece of a resort and therapeutic sanitorium. Guests were drawn there for medical treatments that relied on the healing powers attributed to the mineral-rich hot springs.

Today the geyser is the centerpiece of Hunter's Hot Springs Resort, which uses mineral water from the hot springs (or "hot pots") to fill an outdoor hot mineral pool that is kept at about 104 degrees. Heat from the hot springs is also used to warm the lodge and many guest rooms. A dip in the mineral pool is free for guests of the resort, but a fee is charged for non-guests, who can also use the on-site dressing rooms and shower facilities.

Old Perpetual spouts every ninety seconds—usually.
Cynthia Butterfield

★ ★

Old Perpetual and Hunter's Hot Springs Resort are 2 miles north of Lakeview, on OR 395. The geyser is visible during daylight hours from Geyser View Lane, just off the highway, but it's more fun to park at the resort and walk along the path to the shore of the pond.

For more information about Old Perpetual, call the Lake County Chamber of Commerce at (541) 947-6040 or go to www.lakecounty chamber.org. You can reach Hunter's Hot Springs Resort at (800) 858-8266 or by logging onto www.huntersresort.com.

Monster Magpie
Medford

He's big and goofy and, with those giant claws, can seem a bit ominous. But this 29-foot tall magpie has been a landmark in Medford ever since 1965, when Lee Hobbs first built the bird in hopes of drawing attention, and customers, to his new army surplus store.

Made of concrete reinforcing bars (re-bar) covered with hog wire and a smooth coating of fiberglass, the big-beaked bird roosts permanently in the parking lot of what is now the Black Bird Shopping Center. And over the years the bird has become as much a Medford-mascot as it is a creature of commercialism.

John Hanson, the store employee currently charged with preening the bird, is also the person who helps dress the bird in fun outfits for special occasions. Hanson says that during Medford's annual Pear Blossom Run, the bird sports a tank-top and shorts, and for Christmas the bird gets a Santa hat, big candy cane, and a full, Santa-style beard. "In the past he's had a St. Patrick's Day hat and, for a store anniversary, a birthday party hat and giant bottle of beer. In the old days when we had a children's rodeo in town, we'd give the bird a cowboy hat and a sheriff's badge." It doesn't end there: For Halloween the bird has been dressed up as a witch, and during the local fishing derby, the bird gets it own fishing pole. The only outfit Hanson calls a failure was the Easter bunny costume. "I tried to make the bird into a rabbit, but just could not put rabbit ears on that statue

★ ★

Medford's magpie mascot has been standing
tall for almost fifty years.
Medford CVB

and make it look like anything other than a big black bird."

Medford's magpie sits in the parking lot of the Black Bird Shopping Center at 1810 West Main Street in Medford and can be viewed 24 hours a day. From I-5, take exit 27 towards Medford and head west on Barnett Rd (towards Jacksonville) to Riverside Avenue (OR 99). Turn right and travel north to East Main Street. Turn left and travel for one mile to the Black Bird Shopping Center. For more information, call (541) 779-5431 or see www.blackbirdshoppingcenter.com.

★ ★

Mosquito Festival
Paisley

In petite Paisley (population 240) no one panics when pesky mosquitoes appear. In fact, for years the townspeople bragged that the state's largest mosquitoes were born and bred here.

But that doesn't mean they wanted the big bugs to stick around. It just wasn't easy—or cheap—to get rid of them. Paisley is located on a river, and for a long time stagnant parts of that river and the nearby ponds served as veritable mosquito magnets. There wasn't enough money in the city coffers to pay for cleaning out the river and drying up the ponds. But in 1983, after months of scratching their heads—and their mosquito bites—Paisley promoters hatched plans for a Mosquito Festival to raise funds for mosquito eradication. They organized a parade, a rodeo, a skeet shoot, and an antique, classic, and custom car show. They also held a competition to crown the town's Ms. Quito. And they raised enough money to clean out the river and solve the mosquito problem.

The festival has now become an annual event held on the last full weekend in July. Activities have expanded to include cowboy poetry, a fishing derby, and a fly-in with free camping at the newly paved Paisley Airport.

Paisley is located about 45 miles northwest of Lakeview on OR 31. For more information about the Mosquito Festival, call the City of Paisely at (541) 943-3173.

Hunt for "Diamonds"
Plush

The sunstone was designated as the state gemstone in 1989 and can only be found in Lake County, where rock hounds also hunt for jasper, agates, petrified wood, thunder eggs, and other such earthy delights. Sunstone, also known as aventurine, can occur in any color, but here it is most commonly found in shades of light yellow and amber.

While sunstone is mined commercially, in 1992 a 4-square-mile, free-use sunstone-collecting area was set aside near the tiny town of Plush, prompting locals to dub the sunstone the "Plush diamond."

The Plush sunstone gem field is near Hart Mountain, about 20 miles north of the tiny town of Plush and about 50 miles northeast of Lakeview. For directions and additional information, contact the Lake County Chamber of Commerce at (541) 947-6040 or go to www .lakecountychamber.org.

Cock-a-Doodle Contest
Rogue River

Know a rooster that just won't shut up? Don't throw a shoe at him. Instead, bring him on down to Rogue River for the National Rooster Crowing Contest and let him strut his stuff.

Rogue River has been holding its Rooster Crowing Contest since 1953, after town boosters heard about a similar contest held by coal miners in Wales. That first year so many roosters had something to crow about that the contest was actually staged twice. In the first competition, the $50 cash prize was paid out in silver dollars and went to the owner of Hollerin' Harry, who established the contest record with seventy-one cock-a-doodle-dos in a thirty-minute period. A few months later, Beetle Baum won his owner $100 by crowing 109 times in thirty minutes. That record stood for twenty-five years, until 1978, when a raucous rooster named White Lightning set a new record with 112 crows in half an hour.

"In the early days when there were a lot of farms and farmers," says longtime contest emcee Dave Ehrhardt, "as many as 200 roosters would get entered in the contest. These days not as many people have roosters, and we get perhaps thirty or forty roosters competing for the top prize, which is $150."

There may be some loudmouthed roosters that just naturally go on and on at all times of the day. If the actions and antics of the folks at the contest are any indication, though, some roosters will

The winner of the 2008 Rooster Crow
Contest has something to crow about.
Rogue River Press

only commence to crowing in the afternoon in response to a bit of human cackling, cheering, and cajoling. But all bets are off when you put fifty caged roosters together and ask them to crow on cue. Every year some usually chatty roosters refuse to utter a peep, while other feathered farmhands readily sing out. "Some birds really need something to get them going," say Ehrhardt. "There are people who sing to their birds, talk to them, or blow at them." Whatever it takes.

Each year, before any poultry take the stage, children and adults from the community are invited to step forth for the Human Crow Contest and do a bit of cock-a-doodle-doing on their own. "No cash prizes are awarded," says one longtime festival attendee, "but people get the satisfaction—and I suppose the embarrassment—of being able to tell their friends that they were the warm-up act for a bunch of roosters."

Rogue River is located near I-5, east of Grants Pass. In addition to the Rooster Crowing Contest, the National Rooster Crow Weekend includes a parade, free entertainment, food booths, and a classic car show. For more information contact the Rogue River Chamber of Commerce at (541) 582-0242 or visit www.rrchamber.cc.

On a Tear
Sutherlin

Ed Charon died in April 2007, but if he were around today, he'd tell you not to be afraid of trying new experiences and learning a fresh skill no matter what your age or current occupation. He knew a thing or two about that. That's because in 1988, the retired Roseburg pastor saw someone ripping apart phone books on television and decided to give it a try.

Turns outs that with practice, determination, and a pair of really big hands—he wore a size 16½ ring—Charon got really good at tearing up phone books. He took his skill to schools and prisons, where he'd dramatically rip apart phone books while preaching about clean living and positive life changes.

He also tore up the record books.

In 2002, on his sixty-seventh birthday, Charon set a world record by splitting nineteen telephone directories, each more than 1,000 pages long, in just three minutes. Later that year, he lost the title to someone who tore up thirty directories in three minutes. But Charon clawed his way back to the championship in 2004, when he managed to shred thirty-nine, 1,004-page directories in three minutes.

Charon didn't stop there. He settled in Sutherlin and kept ripping new records. And in late 2006 he won his fifth world record by tearing apart fifty-six Portland phone books (the white pages; 1,006 pages each) in the required three minute time limit. After that, he retired. No doubt to give his phone-book fracturing fingers a well-deserved rest.

Laudable Limbs
Williams

When people would ask the creator of the now-defunct Tree Circus in California how he got his trees to grow in grids, loops, zigzags, ladders, and other surprising shapes, all he would say was that he talked to his trees.

Richard Reames knows better. Inspired by those Circus Trees, which he visited as a child, Reames went out on a limb and devoted his life to the art of shaping living trees into whimsical shapes and functional objects, such as furniture or outdoor rooms. And he discovered that it takes skill, ingenuity, artistic vision, and a lot of coaxing, bending, pruning, and grafting to get trees to do one's bidding. We suspect he probably talks to them as well.

Reames calls his creations "arborsculpture," a blend of art and sculpture that goes beyond bonsai and topiary and even espalier, the technique used to grow fruit trees against walls, on wires, and in small areas. "Arborsculpture is more like espalier on acid," Reames says.

If you could wander through his art studio/nursery in southern Oregon, you'd understand what he means. There are benches made from trees, a spiral staircase growing in an oak, a gazebo made from interlocking birch trees, a tree in the shape of a cello, willows in the shape of hearts, a water spigot growing inside a tree that allows the tree to water itself, and an apple tree that spells out the word love. Reames and a neighbor are even collaborating on a boat that will be harvested in a year or so and set afloat.

In addition to his projects at home, Reames travels around the world planting and shaping trees for public parks and private

Peace endures.
Richard Reames

gardens. And he says it's definitely possible to grow a living, weather-tight house. "Imagine a yard full of trees growing into chairs and tables and beds, mirror frames and coat hangers. There could be a tunnel of live trees leading to the living house where several circles of trees have grown together creating walls and the ceiling, solidly imbedding the doors and windows that function perfectly. Septic and gray water would feed the trees, as would the compost from the kitchen. The insulation value would go up every year as the trees matured, and the trees could also provide fruit or firewood."

While he works out that house idea, Reames enjoys some of his favorite creations, including a peace-sign tree and a chair he's made from an ash tree, because "anytime I want to, I can just go outside and sit on my ash."

Richard Reames's Arborsmith Studios is located in Williams, but it's not open for public tours. However, you can see his creations and photos of sculpted trees from around the world in his books and at www.arborsmith.com.

Lions and Tigers and Bears, Oh My!
Winston

It's a jungle out there, and we're not just talking about the interstate at rush hour.

With 600 acres of grasslands and wooded areas, Wildlife Safari is the only drive-through animal park in the Pacific Northwest. And while parks elsewhere place steep moats between visitors and wild animals, this is the last one in the United States where visitors are allowed to drive their own cars on a safari through the park. So it's easy to motor up to exotic animals from Asia, Africa, and the Americas. In fact, the experience can be so up-close that if you want to see bears, lions, and cheetahs, park regulations won't let you in if you're driving a convertible car, even if you promise to leave the top up.

Seeing camels, emus, tigers, bears, bison, elephants, cheetahs, hippos, giraffes, lions, and other wild beasts just outside your car

★ ★

Be sure to keep your windows rolled up on this safari.
Wildlife Safari

window is definitely exciting. But for an extra fee, the park offers some even wilder if-you-dare activities and experiences. There's Camp Tiki, which begins with an elephant "meet and greet" and ends with an overnight tent-stay inside the elephant yard. Not wild enough? There's also a ranger-led walk through the cheetah area, including some up-close time with Bengal and Siberian tigers. And, for the truly adventurous, there are opportunities to help out during feeding time by joining the rangers as they deliver meals to lions, giraffes, and bears.

Wildlife Safari is open year-round and is located in Winston, about 6 miles south of Roseburg. From I-5 take exit 119 toward Winston. Follow OR 42 for about 2 miles and look for the signs. Admission is charged. Some special activities, such as lion and bear feedings, require additional fees and may have height or age restrictions. For more information call (541) 679-6761 or visit www.wildlifesafari.org.

6

Columbia River Gorge and Central Oregon

Windsurfers, hikers, bikers, climbers, skiers, spelunkers, and their ilk flock to this part of the state for fun and frivolity. So do curiosity seekers en route to what may be the World's Oldest Slice of Wedding Cake, a singing bridge, a field where pears grow in glass bottles, and the farm that pioneered artificial turkey insemination.

Elsewhere, four acres of curious installations at Bend's Funny Farm, including a bowling ball tree, a pink flamingo nesting area, and a heart-shaped pond with a giant arrow stuck in the middle (the Love Pond), are endlessly entertaining. The table at Parkdale's Hutson Museum set with slabs of meat, a bowl of potatoes, bread, butter, and a brimming cup of coffee—all made of inedible rocks and minerals—is confounding. And in Redmond, the whimsical, patriotic, and magical sculptures made from petrified wood, agate, jasper, lava and obsidian at Petersen Rock Garden are just plain enchanting.

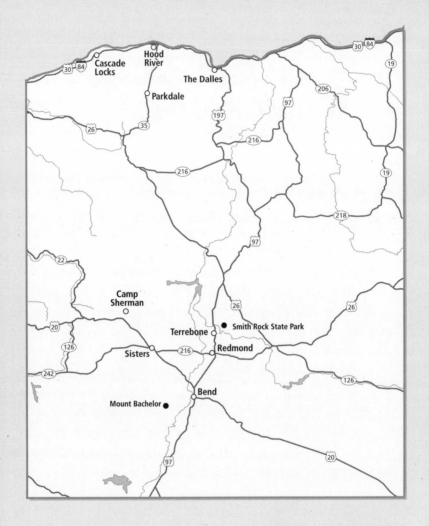

Columbia River Gorge & Central Oregon

★ ★

It's a Bird! It's a Plane! No, It's a Lawn Chair!
Bend

Kent Couch is a guy who's always had his head in the clouds.

When he was a kid, he'd always wonder what it would be like to fly. As an adult, he found out, by taking to the sky in a most curious way.

Couch's light bulb moment came while watching a TV show about Larry Walters, a truck driver who became somewhat of a folk hero back in 1982 after flying over Los Angeles in a lawn chair rigged up with helium balloons.

Couch decided to give that a try. But instead of simply flying over a city, his goal was to fly a balloon-powered lawn chair from his

There are no traffic jams here.
Smart Solutions–Bend

home in central Oregon across the state line into Idaho, more than 200 miles away.

It took him three tries. He had to parachute out of his first try in 2006. On his second try, in 2007, he stayed aloft for 193 miles and touched down in northeastern Oregon, a bit shy of the state line. His third try, on July 5, 2008, was a success. On that day, Couch took off early in the morning from the parking lot of his Bend gas station seated in a lawn chair with more than 150 giant, brightly-colored, helium-filled balloons tied to it. For ballast, the chair was rigged with three water barrels filled with cherry Kool-Aid. For safety, Couch had a GPS device, a satellite phone, and a BB gun so he could shoot out balloons and control his altitude. He also wore a parachute, just in case something went wrong.

Luckily, all went well. Couch floated east for nine hours and twelve minutes, at an average speed of 26 miles per hour, and at altitudes that topped out at 16,625 feet. When he finally touched down, it was in Cambridge, Idaho, 240 miles away. Couch had not only reached his goal, he'd set a world distance record for cluster ballooning.

You can learn more about Kent Couch and his record-setting lawn chair flight at www.couchballoons.com.

Down on the Fun Farm
Bend

Gene Carsey owns about twenty acres of land just off the highway between Bend and Redmond and, so far, he's filled four acres of his fields and many of the farm buildings with whimsical folk art sculptures and just enough downright curious stuff to make the Fun Farm, well, just plain fun.

For starters, there's Carsey himself. He's been collecting odds and ends for about thirty years now. There's a house full of antiques and secondhand furniture he'd be happy to sell and packets of bowling ball seeds or, to use their proper name, Gloriosa Strike-a-Bunda. But

"The Twins" are always ready to roll at the Fun Farm.
Ross Reynolds

Carsey says he's mostly interested in puttering around and creating more fun stuff for visitors to encounter. In fact, when we stopped by, the yard and the shop were wide open, but Carsey was nowhere to be found—though we did come upon a pair of bright yellow diving flippers in the pathway beside a pile of freshly-cut tree limbs.

Stuff like that isn't a bit unusual when you consider what else is out in the fields. There's the Pink Flamingo Nesting Area, and a telephone pole decorated with old rotary telephones. There's also a

★ ★

yellow brick road, some goats, and the off-kilter replica of the house that dropped on one of the witches from *The Wizard of Oz*. And there are bowling balls galore: a Bowling Ball Garden, a Bowling Ball Shrine, and a tree sprouting bowling balls instead of leaves. (Looks like those bowling ball seeds really work!) And then there are "The Twins," a conjoined mannequin with three legs, two heads, two arms, and one bowling ball.

For folks who get overwhelmed by all this, Carsey has created the contemplative Love Pond. You can't miss it: It's in the shape of a heart with a red path around it and a giant Cupid's arrow stuck in the middle. "You're supposed to sing 'Love Me Tender' as you walk around it," says Carsey. "And if you're planning to get married, come by on the third Saturday in June. That's when I hire a preacher and we have our annual Free Wedding Day." Sounds like fun.

The Fun Farm is at 64990 Deschutes Market Road in Bend, just east of US 97. To get there, go north from Bend on US 97 and turn right on Deschutes Market Road. You'll end up facing the Fun Farm barn. For more information call (541) 389-6391.

Deep-rooted Restaurant
Bend

This landmark restaurant, in operation since 1936, overlooks Mirror Pond and the Deschutes River in downtown Bend. It's also known for its honey butter and scones and for the curious fact that there are two trees in the center of the dining room. One is a 250-year-old Ponderosa pine that rises right up through a hole in the ceiling.

The Pine Tavern is at 967 Northwest Brooks in Bend. From OR 97 South, go past Revere Avenue and turn right on Greenwood Avenue. Turn left onto Wall Street and then take a right onto Oregon Street, where you'll see the restaurant. For hours and more information call (541) 382-5581 or see www.pinetavern.com.

Hungry? Try tree-side dining.
Heidi Lagao, Kolshots Photography; Kolshots.com

★ ★

Seatbelts Required for This Art Tour
Bend

Plenty of cities have roundabouts, or traffic circles, at many street intersections. Sign-studded and usually made of concrete or planted with scrubby greenery, the roundabouts calm down traffic and usually leave it at that.

Not in Bend. There the roundabouts don't just sit there being round. Using matching funds from the city's public art program, at least sixteen roundabouts (so far) have sprouted amusing and entertaining art. The sculptures form an outdoor, drive-by art gallery and portray everything from a giant, lacy steel orb and a flock of migrating steel birds to a grizzly bear, a big bronze logger, and a school of flying fish.

Native redside trout by Miles Pepper swim with the wind at this roundabout.
James Goodchap/Visit Bend

Want to see them all? There's an on-line gallery at www.artin publicplaces.org. But it will really be more fun to print out a map, fill up the gas tank, buckle-up, head out on the road, and circle a few of Bend's curious traffic circles.

Bearly There

Bend

Located near the geographic center of Oregon, the city of Bend (once known as Farewell Bend) has grown from a rough-and-rugged timber boomtown to the most cosmopolitan city east of the Cascades. The saloons and sawmills may now be replaced by fine restaurants and

Bend can boast a Smokey Bear original.

theaters, but that doesn't mean the streets don't clear for the annual July Fourth Pet Parade, when children, adults, and pets such as dogs, llamas, horses, lizards, goats, and a good number of stuffed animals parade through the downtown streets.

Animals are also on hand year-round at the High Desert Museum, which has oodles of indoor and outdoor exhibits exploring the wildlife, living history, and landscapes of eight western states. The historical artifacts are top notch, but most folks are surprised to encounter more than a hundred live creatures including bats, barn owls, river otters, porcupines, scorpions, toads, salmon, gray foxes, golden eagles, lizards, snakes, and spiders.

The museum's countdown of critters also includes one of the earliest Smokey Bear costumes. A longtime symbol for fire prevention, Smokey was only a poster bear until 1950 when a four-month-old black bear was rescued in New Mexico after a forest fire and given the name Smokey. A year later Smokey Bear costumes and toys started popping up everywhere. And according to the forestry worker who showed up at the museum with the vintage costume, this particular Smokey outfit first appeared in the 1952 Macy's Thanksgiving Day Parade in New York City before making its way west.

The High Desert Museum is at 59800 South OR 97, 7 miles south of downtown Bend. For more information call (541) 382-4754 or visit www.highdesertmuseum.org.

Curious Caves
Bend

Spelunking, or cave exploration, is a popular activity around Bend, and it's a great way to find out about some of the curious stuff tucked away underground. Even some of the cave names and former cave uses are quite curious.

Skeleton Cave, for example, was named for the fossils and modern bones found near the cave entrance. And before there was electricity, ice was "mined" from the recesses of the Arnold Ice Caves. But

* ★

Trivia

Lots-o-Lava Lore

- On the trail that circles the 150-foot-deep crater on Lava Butte, look for kipukas, small oasis-like islands of green trees growing in the black lava.

- According to the Forest Service, the volume of rock in the Lava Butte lava flow is 380,000,000 cubic yards. That much rock, they figure, would pave 160,000 miles of road 24 feet wide and 6 inches thick. That road would be long enough to circle around the world six and a half times.

- That imaginary road would be a bit longer if some of the lava here hadn't been removed. In 1929 about 2,000 cubic yards of lava cinders from the butte were trucked to Bend, loaded into railcars, and shipped to Longview, Washington. There the cinders were used to make concrete for a bridge across the Columbia River to Oregon.

the most unusual, and accessible, cave around here is the mile-long Lava River Cave, Oregon's longest intact lava tube. Trapper Leander Dillman discovered this cave in 1889, and in the following years he used it to cool his venison. It's now part of the Newberry National Volcanic Monument and can be explored with lanterns, flashlights, warm clothes, and good walking shoes. Those who venture into the cave will pass Collapsed Corridor, which is dotted with piles of volcanic rock, and Two Tube Tunnel, which is a cave inside a cave. There's also the 50-foot-wide Echo Hall, where the 58-foot-high ceiling transforms conversations into strange noises.

Above ground the nearby landscape is just as eerie. A few miles south of the Lava River Cave is the Lava Cast Forest, a Pompeii-like place created 6,000 years ago when lava enveloped living trees, hardened, and then left behind molds of those trees. And back at the Lava Lands Visitor Center, an observation tower and an interpretive trail offer views of and access to the 500-foot-high Lave Butte, a cinder cone that erupted 7,000 year ago, leaving behind a bizarre-looking 9-square-mile lava field that is 30 to 100 feet thick.

To explore this area, it's a good idea to start at the Lava Lands Visitor Center, which is 11 miles south of Bend on US 97. There you can get maps, see exhibits about the volcanic history of the area, join a guided walk, or rent the lantern you'll need to explore the Lava River Cave. For more information call (541) 593-2421 or go to www.fs.fed.us/r6/centraloregon/newberrynvm.

Birth of a River
Camp Sherman

The scenic Metolius River is one of the largest spring-fed rivers in the United States. Designated a National Wild and Scenic River in 1988, the upper end of the waterway is popular with fly-fishing fans. Farther downstream, the rushing waters are a big hit with white-water rafting enthusiasts. But the curious among us will be drawn to the Head of the Metolius River.

Geologists believe the river is fed by underground springs that originate beneath nearby Black Butte or perhaps by springs in the Cascade Mountains to the west. Either way, the river can be seen gushing directly from the hillside at full force, at about 50,000 gallons a minute, pretty much year-round. It's an unusual sight, made a bit more unusual by the fact that it's so easy to get to.

Want to see for yourself? The Head of the Metolius is about 11 miles north-northwest of Sisters. From Sisters head 9.6 miles west on US 20 and go about 4.5 miles north on Forest Service Road 14 toward Camp Sherman. Park at the Head of the Metolius day use

It's not every day that you get to see a river being born.
Ross Reynolds

site, and head out along the quarter-mile paved path that leads to a railing and scenic view point that overlooks the water.

Herman the Sturgeon

Cascade Locks

There's plenty of entertainment at the visitor center on the Oregon side of the Bonneville Dam, the first of eight lock-and-dam projects to be built in the 1930s on the Columbia River. You can tour the power-generating facilities, learn from the exhibits, look out over the fish ladders or take the long elevator ride down to the fish-viewing windows, and, depending on the season, see salmon, lamprey eels, or other river residents swim by.

But by far the most curious attraction is next door at the Sturgeon Viewing and Interpretive Center at the Bonneville Fish Hatchery. This is

★ ★

where Herman the Sturgeon lives, an ugly-but-sort-of-lovable 10-foot-long white sturgeon who weighs in at more than 400 pounds.

White sturgeons are the largest freshwater fish in North America. They belong to an ancient group of fish that appeared in the Jurassic period and can grow to be 20 feet long, weigh more than 1,500 pounds, and live for more than one hundred years. So at only about sixty years old, Herman is just a middle-aged fish with a long life ahead of him.

Or so we hope.

Herman I made regular appearances at the Oregon State Fair from 1935 to the mid-1980s. But in 1985 he was stolen from his home at the hatchery in the middle of the night and was never heard from again. Herman II got sick at the State Fair (too many corn dogs, maybe?) and died soon after returning home to the hatchery. Herman III came to the interpretive center in December 1998 and seems to be doing quite well, though plans are under way to bring him back to the State Fair. So you never know.

You can visit the current Herman the Sturgeon at the Sturgeon Viewing and Interpretive Center at the Bonneville Fish Hatchery, 70543 Northeast Herman Loop, in Cascade Locks. From I-84 take exit 40 and follow the signs to the fish hatchery. For hours and more information contact the Bonneville Fish Hatchery at (541) 374-8393 or swim to www.dfw.state.or.us/resources/visitors/bonneville_hatchery.asp.

A Piece of Cake
Hood River

Many newlyweds follow tradition and save a portion of their wedding cake to eat on their first anniversary. It sounds romantic, but since traditional cakes usually don't taste so good after being frozen for a year, bakers often supply a special top layer that can survive a year on ice.

At some weddings you'll find a groom's cake in addition to the traditional multitiered wedding cake. In the past, the groom's cake, traditionally a dark fruitcake, was saved and shared with the newlyweds

Baked in 1887, this is possibly the world's
oldest piece of wedding cake.
Ross Reynolds

after their honeymoon, or slices were given to unmarried girls to place
under their pillows so they'd dream of their future husbands. These
days, though, if there is a groom's cake it's often sliced and boxed and
sent home with wedding guests as a sweet memento of the event.

You might find yourself pondering the tradition while studying the
piece of cake on display at the Hood River County Historical Museum.
Sitting on a dainty paper doily in its own small, delicate glass case,
this piece of fruitcake dates to 1887, when Jennie Boynton married
Joseph Shoemaker in Pendleton, Oregon. The cake survived the couple's move to Hood River in 1889 and outlasted Joseph and Jennie,
who died in 1922 and 1936 respectively. For some reason the cake
was kept and, in 1963, it was given to the museum for safekeeping.

Museum coordinator Connie Nice suspects the cake may have
lasted so long in part because "like traditional fruitcakes, it may be
laced with a great deal of alcohol." And now that the cake is well

over a hundred years old, it has attained a level of celebrity status around town. "Part of the reason we keep it is because of the strong tie to the Shoemaker family, who were pioneers in this area," says Nice. "It's been part of several different museum displays, and we once took it downtown to an event and let people guess how old it was. No one came close."

The cake made in 1887 for Jennie and Joseph's wedding is on display at the Hood River County Historical Museum at 300 East Port Marina Drive in Hood River. For directions and hours call (541) 386-6772 or visit www.co.hood-river.or.us/museum.

Fruit Loop
Hood River

The Columbia River Gorge is the nation's largest pear-growing region and home to a multitude of orchards, wineries, and farms that raise everything from alpacas to lavender. A fun way to explore the area is to drive along the scenic 35-mile "Fruit Loop" that meanders through the Hood River Valley, where plenty of wineries and farms offer tours and free samples.

Go in August and you might get a special treat: a glimpse of mature pears growing inside bottles hanging on the trees at McCurdy Farms in Oak Grove.

This unusual crop is used to make the award-winning *Eau-de-Vie de Poire* (pear brandy with a pear in the bottle) at the Clear Creek Distillery in Portland. What's the secret to getting those pears in the bottles? "No secret," says Craig McCurdy, one of the orchard owners, "just hard work." And the lessons learned from the folks in parts of Europe who have been doing this for hundreds of years. Here, each May, 2,500 bottles are placed on pear trees in the McCurdy orchards, when the pears are small enough to fit through the neck of a bottle. (That's the "secret.") Then, each August, the mature pears in their bottles are harvested and trucked to the distillery in Portland. There the bottles are cleaned and filled with the pear brandy the

Physics trumps Mother Nature.
Jim Lomasson

company is well known for producing. It's a time-consuming and not-yet-perfected process: Up to 30 percent of the bottled-pear crop is lost each year, and it takes about thirty pounds of pears to make the brandy that goes into each bottle. This helps explain why the price tag for this specialty item hovers at more than $70 a bottle.

Want to see—and taste—for yourself? Free Fruit Loop maps are available throughout the Hood River Valley and at the Hood River Visitor's Center on I-84 at exit 63. McCurdy Farms, just one of the stops on the Fruit Loop, is located at 2000 Tucker Road in Hood River. The pear-in-a-bottle brandy is available at their fruit stand, which is open daily from mid-August to November 1. The Clear Creek Distillery, which makes a variety of fruit brandies as well as a single-malt whiskey, has a tasting room in Portland, at 2389 Northwest Wilson Street. For hours and directions call (503) 248-9470 or visit www.clearcreekdistillery.com.

★ ★

Singing Bridge
Hood River

Built in 1924 to replace ferry service on the Columbia River between Hood River and White Salmon, Washington, the straightforwardly named Hood River–White Salmon Interstate Bridge is a mile-long structure with a song in its heart.

It wasn't always so. Until 1950 the bridge had a wood decking system that did little more than creak as cars streamed across it. But when the Port of Hood River purchased the bridge, it replaced the wood deck with steel grating. After that folks began noticing a new, much more pleasant sound from car wheels rushing over the grooved deck. "Everyone started calling it the Singing Bridge," explains a woman who crosses the bridge twice each day on her way to and from work, "but really it's more of a steady humming that's really sort of cool."

Listen closely: This bridge sings.
Ross Reynolds

Like many others, this woman makes sure to open her car windows when crossing the bridge, so she can hear the humming. "But I make sure to keep my elbows inside. We may have new steel decking, but the lanes on the bridge are still very narrow, just 10 feet across."

Have a song in your heart—or your tires? You can belt it out on the Hood River–White Salmon Interstate Bridge, aka the Singing Bridge, by taking exit 64 from I-84. Then, if you're coming from the west, take a left; if you're coming from the east, take a right. You'll end up at the bridge toll plaza: the cost is 75 cents per car to cross the bridge.

Chew Hard
Parkdale

The volunteers who staff Parkdale's Hutson Museum are delighted when visitors stop by. But they don't want you to get the wrong idea: That hearty meal set out on the lace tablecloth isn't for you.

No need to be offended. The yummy-looking slabs of meat, the bowl of potatoes, the plate of bread and butter, and the brimming cup of coffee are actually not food at all. They're specially chosen rocks and minerals that look exactly like food—especially when set out on fine china.

Locals who remember Jesse and Winifred Hutson say the "dinner" is just an example of the couple's good humor and of how much they knew and loved their collection, which included not only thousands of carefully selected rocks, but also an array of unusual personal mementos, significant Native American artifacts, pioneer hand tools, and heavy equipment.

That collection is now the core of the Hutson Museum, which sits on a two-acre complex in the center of Parkdale. Located at the end of the 22-mile Mount Hood Railroad line, the complex includes an orchard, historic farm buildings, and the curious sign illustrated below that informs visitors about an important milestone in the history of turkey sandwiches.

It looks appetizing, but this rocky meal
would really sit heavy in your stomach.
Doris Hill

WORLD HISTORY

APPROXIMATELY 100 FEET SOUTH-
EAST OF THIS SIGN, DAVID R. COOPER
(COOPER SPUR), FIRST ARTIFICIALLY
INSEMINATED A TURKEY...
...FROM THIS EXPERIMENT THE
WORLD NOW HAS THE:
BROAD BREASTED TURKEY

This shrine is meant for turkey
sandwich fans.
Ross Reynolds

The Hutson Museum is open seasonally and is located at 4967 Baseline Drive in Parkdale, about 17 miles from Hood River. To get there take OR 35 south to Hood River Highway/Cooper Spur Road and turn right on Baseline Drive/Hood River Highway. For more information call (541) 352-6808.

Rudolph's Retreat

Redmond

Santa, Mrs. Claus, and the elves may be happy spending twelve months a year bundled up in the frigid North Pole. Not Rudolph. Not Prancer. Not Blitzen. And not their reindeer friends.

Except for that Christmas Eve gig and a few special events around the holiday season, it turns out that Santa's reindeer spend most of the year lounging around with a herd of other domesticated reindeer at a ranch in Redmond called Operation Santa Claus.

Established in 1950 with a few reindeer from Alaska, Operation Santa Claus was for a long time the largest herd of domesticated reindeer in the United States. At its peak the farm had more than 120 reindeer, many of which could be rented in small groups for guest appearances at shopping malls, parties, and fairs. The herd is much smaller these days, ranging from just a dozen to somewhere around forty reindeer, depending on the season, but there is always a small contingent at home to greet visitors.

Although the owners of Operation Santa Claus have full-time jobs off-site, visitors are welcome to stop by any day of the year, during daylight hours, and take a self-guided tour of the reindeer at rest. "But please," the ranch owner told us, "tell people to stay on the gravel path and not to climb over the fences or open any gates. You can't imagine what we have to go through when reindeer get loose."

And just in case you're wondering, reindeer are definitely real, not just some animal made up for the Christmas stories. But no, they don't really fly.

At least not while anyone is looking.

Rest stop for reindeers.

Operation Santa Claus is open year-round and is located 2 miles west of Redmond, at 4355 West OR 126. For more information call the ranch at (541) 548-8910 or contact the Redmond Chamber of Commerce at (541) 923-5191.

★ ★

Rock On!

Redmond

An often overlooked but true folk art wonder, the Petersen Rock Garden and Museum is a must-see fairyland. And from the looks of it, you'd better hurry. The whimsical, patriotic, and just darn magical rock sculptures Rasmus Petersen created on his farm back in the late 1930s and throughout the 1940s look a little worse for wear and

Rasmus Petersen made magical art from simple stone.
Ross Reynolds

★ ★

structural inattention. But in some ways that just increases the appeal of this place.

Back in 1935, not long after Petersen put his 300-acre farm into operation, he turned his attention to his yard. Not content with just hauling in some boulders for a rock wall and creating simple flower beds, he built a small rockery next to his house.

Then, well, it looks as if things got out of hand. The farmer-turned-artist went into the nearby hills and mountains and hauled home rocks that he used to build ornate castles. He made rock ponds that, of course, needed rock bridges to take people across them. He assembled miniature rock churches, laid out a rock U.S. flag, and worked with a local sculptor to turn a giant boulder into a replica of the Statue of Liberty.

Petersen's materials? Tons of petrified wood, agate, jasper, thundereggs, lava, and obsidian that he gathered within an 85-mile radius of his farm. And he never got tired of all the hard work.

Rasmus Petersen died in 1952, but family members keep the sculpture garden open to the public. If you go, bring a picnic and a camera and keep an eye out for the peacocks, ducks, and chickens that make their home among the rock art. Be sure to visit the small on-site museum as well, because inside there's a wonderful display of fluorescent rocks.

The Petersen Rock Garden and Museum is open daily and is located 7 miles southwest of US 97 at 7930 Southwest Seventy-seventh Street in Redmond. Admission is collected on the honor system; there's a wooden box in the parking lot. For more information call (541) 382–5574.

Oh, Brother!
Sisters

This quaint, Western-themed town on the east side of the Cascade Mountains gets its name from the three mountain peaks that can be seen in the southwest skyline. Individually known as Faith, Hope, and

"Smile when you look at me, pardner."

Charity, the trio is collectively called the Three Sisters. Back in the 1880s, Three Sisters seemed like a great name for the tiny town, but postal authorities apparently thought the name was a tad too long and instead shortened the name to Sisters when the post office was moved here from 3 miles up the road.

Sisters' fortunes have ebbed and flowed over the years. In the late nineteenth century, ranchers herding bands of sheep to their summer grazing lands often passed through town. The smell left behind was said to last for weeks. In the 1920s two separate fires threatened to wipe out the former lumber-producing town, but resourceful locals dug in and rebuilt. In fact, the town's first jail had bars made from the spokes of old iron buggy wheels and was once mentioned in *Ripley's Believe It Or Not!* as being the only known jail to have never housed a prisoner.

These days pretty much every building in Sisters—new or old—has a Western-style facade. One of the town's few original buildings, the circa 1912 Hotel Sisters, is now the home of Bronco Billy's Ranch Grill and Saloon. Sidle up to an old-timer in the bar and it's a good bet that within a few minutes you'll hear stories of the ghost of the woman in an old-style dress who's been seen on the steps and look-ing out of the upstairs windows late at night when the doors were locked up tight. "She scared one of our janitors half to death," says one waiter, "and now no one wants to be here alone on clean-up duty after a late-night party anymore."

Bronco Billy's Ranch Grill and Saloon is in downtown Sisters, at 190 East Cascade Street; phone (541) 549-7427. For information about events in Sisters, such as the Sisters Rodeo and Parade held each June and the Outdoor Quilt Show each July, contact the Sisters Area Chamber of Commerce at (541) 549-0251 or visit www.sisters chamber.com.

Monkey Face
Terrebonne

In central Oregon's high desert plateau, the 650-acre Smith Rock State Park draws hikers and climbers from around the world. There are miles of hiking and biking trails and more than 1,400 climbing routes on this 550-foot-tall hunk of compressed volcanic ash, but by far the most popular and well-known climb is Monkey Face, a 350-foot spire that looks exactly like the face of a monkey, complete with a monkey mouth big enough to stand up in.

Monkey Face's fame may have inspired and challenged climbers

The 350-foot Monkey Face is a favorite spot for climbers.
Oregon Parks and Recreation Department

to be creative in naming some of the other climbs in the park. Or perhaps it was a result of high-altitude giddiness. How else to explain climbing routes and areas dubbed the Moons of Pluto, Screaming Yellow Zonkers, Tammy Bakker's Face, Gumby, Wooden Ships, Exile on Main Street, Gimme Shelter, Taco Chips, Spiderman Buttress, Cocaine Gully, Pleasure Palace, Wombat, and Kangaroo?

Smith Rock State Park is located 2 miles east of Terrebonne, off Northeast Wilcox Avenue. For more information call (541) 548-7501 or visit www.smithrock.com or www.oregonstateparks.org/park_51.php.

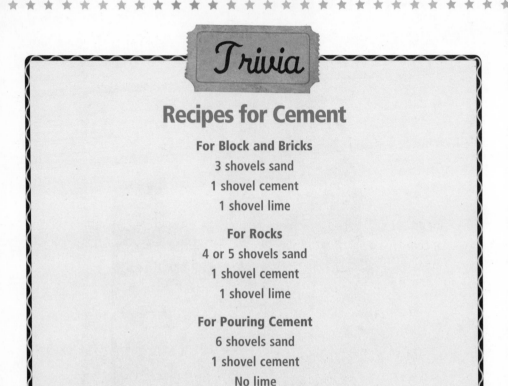

Trivia

Recipes for Cement

For Block and Bricks
3 shovels sand
1 shovel cement
1 shovel lime

For Rocks
4 or 5 shovels sand
1 shovel cement
1 shovel lime

For Pouring Cement
6 shovels sand
1 shovel cement
No lime

Recipes courtesy Juanita Bright

Rock Castles
The Dalles

According to Juanita Bright, when her dad, Ira McKissen, visited Redmond's Petersen Rock Garden and Museum sometime in the early 1980s, he was mighty impressed by the rock sculptures he saw there depicting everything from the Statue of Liberty to a lovely little church. But, she says, it was Petersen's rock castles that spurred her dad into action once he got home: "He started collecting rocks here in Oregon and on his trips to Arizona. Then he got a rock saw and starting cutting the rocks himself, and then he filled the terraces in his backyard in Rowena with almost a dozen rock castles, one on each terrace."

★ ★

Ira McKissen is gone, and these days a friend of the family tends the terraced castles. But Juanita wanted a few of those castles for her own yard, so she arranged to have them moved to the roadside outside her home on the Historic Columbia River Highway (US 30) about 5 miles west of The Dalles.

Bright has also kept hold of her dad's instructions for making and mixing the cement he used to keep his rock castles together. And she says she keeps the recipes with her cookbooks just in case she needs to whip up a batch of cement to make a repair. "The amount needed for any project depends on the size of the project and the amount of cement a person uses," says Bright. "Some people use more and some less; I usually use more because I enjoy using it."

Ira McKissen's castles were labors of love.

★ ★

So That's How They Did It!
The Dalles

Watch any old Western movie and it's a given there'll be a scene
or two set in a saloon with a slew of wranglers lined up at the bar.
In front of each grizzled drinker will be a shot glass and a bottle of
whiskey. Sure, it's a movie, but as those cowboys threw back shot
after shot, did you ever wonder how they could drink so much and
still be standing? Or alert and coordinated enough to go for their
guns and engage in the inevitable shoot-out with the new sheriff in
town or that stranger striding through the swinging doors?

Attentive visitors to the Columbia Gorge Discovery Center and
Museum are let in on what may be a true Old West secret. If you
don't want to know, skip to the next entry now.

Set 'Em Up! After being stored away for many
years, the bar from the Umatilla House
is back in service. You can visit it in the
lounge at the Columbia Portage Grill in The Dalles. While the "trick"
bar counter is long gone, the intricately carved mahogany bar back
is still around, with its original cherubs and pair of 5-foot-tall carved
ladies affectionately dubbed the "Twin Virgins."

The Columbia Portage Grill is located inside the Shilo Hotel and
Suites at 3223 Bret Clodfelter Way in The Dalles. For more information
call (541) 298-3287.

★ ★

In a museum filled with everything from rare, woven Native American baskets to an impressive collection of 1,200-plus padlocks, there's one room with a great display of more than a dozen different types of barbed wire and, beside it, a replica of the solid mahogany bar from the historic Umatilla House. Built in 1857, this lavish inn in The Dalles was known as the best hotel west of the Mississippi. It burned down in 1887, but was rebuilt and continued operation as a hotel, restaurant and bar, and later an apartment house, until it was dismantled in 1929.

When it was in its prime, though, the Umatilla House was the place to be. The dining room seated 250 people, and there were 123 rooms with a stove in each one. But strangers who went to the bar had to watch out for tricksters.

According to a note posted in the museum, the bar offered regular customers not just a ledge to lean on, but an edge on staying vertical while drinking. One former hotel owner revealed the trick: "Under the molding, approximately eighteen inches apart, is a series of augured holes. The holes were used by men while drinking at the bar to keep their balance. While one man would dare the other in a drinking spree, he could stand erect longer and drink more if he could place his fingers in the augured holes to steady his weaving body."

Bartender, a round on me!

The Columbia Gorge Discovery Center and Museum is located at 5000 Discovery Avenue Drive in The Dalles. To get there from I-84, take exit 82 toward Columbia Gorge Discovery Center/Wasco County Museum. If coming from the west, turn right (left if coming from the east) on Chenoweth Road, right on US 30 and right again onto Discovery Drive. For more information call (541) 296-8600 or go to www.gorgediscovery.org.

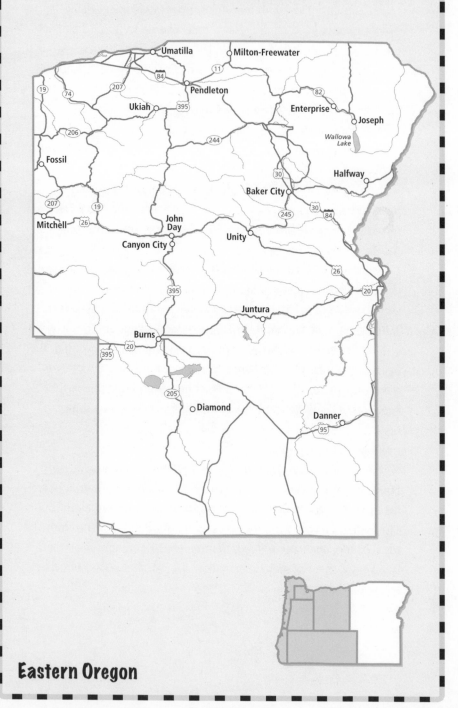

Eastern Oregon

7

Eastern Oregon

*E*astern Oregon is definitely the wild side of the state. Out here you'll find Hells Canyon, the country's deepest river gorge, as well as the World's Largest Mushroom, a herd of rare wild mustangs, and annual competitions involving mules, ground squirrels and jumping frogs. It's the part of the state where jailed inmates can earn money sewing a sought-after brand of blue jeans marketed under the slogan "Made on the Inside to be Worn on the Outside." And since 1910 it's been home to one of the country's oldest and most famous rodeos, the Pendleton Round-Up, an event that has its own brand of whiskey and its own Hall of Fame, where visitors are greeted by War Paint, a taxidermied bucking horse once considered to be the greatest saddle bronc of all time. Keep the pony saddled, because in Baker City there's a display of gold that includes gold buttons and a nugget weighing in at more than 80 ounces and worth, last we checked, more than $76,000. In Burns they've got a giant ball of string that tips the scales at 265 pounds. Over in Canyon City, there's a museum with several taxidermied two-headed calves and the skulls of the first two people hanged locally. In Fossil, there are public fossil beds at the high school where you can dig for prehistoric treasure. And in Joseph you'll be smart to watch out for Wally, a horned, multi-legged, bovine-like water beast that may—or may not—live in Wallowa Lake.

★ ★

Fresh Maine Lobster and Green Turtle Soup
Baker City

Built in 1889 during the gold-mining boom that transformed Baker City into the "Queen City of the Mines," the Geiser Grand Hotel was the place to be and be seen, and the place to go to spend some of the wealth acquired from area gold mines. Built in the ornate Italianate Renaissance Revival style and designed by an architect who went on to become the first post–WWII president of Czechoslovakia, the Geiser was one of the first hotels in Oregon to have electricity and the third hotel west of the Mississippi to have an elevator. (The Hotel Jerome in Aspen and the Hotel Del Coronado in San Diego had the first and second Otis elevators.)

During its heyday the hotel hosted timber and cattle barons, mine owners, bankers, and dignitaries such as Teddy Roosevelt. And they all sat down to eat in the Geiser Grand's Palm Court, where white-gloved, tuxedo-clad waiters served dishes from an eclectic menu that included fresh bear steak, green turtle soup, Maine lobster, and New York ice cream that had been whisked across country in refrigerated rail cars.

When the gold mines closed, economic hard times set in, but the Geiser Grand held on until 1968. The final guests were the cast of the movie *Paint Your Wagon*, which was being filmed in Baker County and which, ironically, portrayed a rollicking "No Name City" that was much like Baker City in its glory days. After that the building fell into disrepair and was almost demolished to make way for a parking lot.

A $7 million restoration brought the hotel back to its former self in 1997. Staircases and ornate architectural details were restored, the magnificent stained-glass ceiling in the Palm Court is once again the largest in the Northwest, and now all guest rooms have private baths.

But not everything has been made perfect. Sharp-eyed guests in the hotel's saloon will notice a bullet hole over the left eye of the restored tin lion's head. The hole is a reminder of the days when

Paint Your Wagon was filmed here.
Geiser Grand Hotel

★ ★

Baker City was a true Wild West town, the sort of place where cowboys and miners finished a night of drinking by stumbling down the street and aiming their six-shooters at the decorative faces on the clock tower outside the hotel.

The Geiser Grand is located at 1996 Main Street in downtown Baker City. For more information call (888) 434-7474 or visit www.geisergrand.com.

Old Gold

Baker City

Once a stop along the old Oregon Trail, the frontier town of Baker City was transformed into a hub of social, cultural, and economic activity in 1861 when Henry Griffin discovered gold nearby and set off an eastern Oregon gold rush.

Under the Grand

As in much of the American West, Chinese workers played an important role in Baker County. They worked in the gold mines, built mining ditches and railroads, and provided other services to the community. In the late 1800s and early 1900s, Baker City's "China Town" had a half-dozen stores, a temple, a gambling establishment, and links to a network of tunnels that ran underneath the city sidewalks.

Today visitors exploring on their own or as part of the regular Sunday-afternoon tours at the Geiser Grand Hotel can peer into those tunnels from the Historic Cellar, where large mahogany-framed windows mark the tunnel entrances.

★ ★

The 80.4-ounce Armstrong nugget is displayed in a bank lobby.
Debi Bainter

Today the downtown historic district boasts more than one hundred commercial and residential buildings on the National Register of Historic Places. A walking-tour pamphlet points out the gems, but most everyone makes a beeline to the U.S. Bank. Not to use the ATM, necessarily, but to lay eyes on the gold on display in the lobby. There, outshining the gold flakes, the gold buttons, and gold nuggets that look tiny by comparison, is the Armstrong Gold Nugget. Weighing in at 80.4 ounces, the nugget was discovered in June 1913 by George Armstrong as he walked behind his son out of a placer mine near Susanville, Oregon. Back in 1913 the nugget was worth about $1,400. Today a rock like this might fetch more than $76,000.

To see the gold display, head to the U.S. Bank at 2000 Main Street weekdays during normal business hours. For more information contact the Baker County Chamber of Commerce at (800) 523-1235.

Filmed Here

In 1968 Baker County had a part as the stand-in for gold-rush-era California in the 1969 film version of the Broadway musical comedy *Paint Your Wagon*. If you watch the movie, look closely and you'll see bits and pieces of the landscape around here on-screen behind Lee Marvin, (a singing!) Clint Eastwood, and Jean Sebert.

Sets for "No Name City" were built about 42 miles outside of Baker City, but they were destroyed shortly after the movie was made. However, a model of the fictional town is on display at the Oregon Trail Regional Museum at 2480 Grove Street in downtown Baker City, which is open daily May through October. For more information call (541) 523-9308.

Debi Bainter

★ ★

Mr. Baker City
Baker City

In 1904 there was no way to tell that the nine-year-old kid selling
magazines from a paper bag would grow up to have a seven-state
magazine distribution empire that sold more than three million magazines a year. But Leo Adler clearly had an uncanny business sense and
a dogged determination: When the self-made millionaire died at the
age of ninety-eight, his estate was worth millions.

Throughout his long life, "Mr. Baker City," as Adler was affectionately known, maintained a surprisingly modest lifestyle. He never
moved out of the two-story, Italianate-style Baker City home his family
moved into in 1899. A lifelong bachelor, Adler never installed electricity
on the second story of his home and simply closed that floor off when
his mother died in the 1930s. And during the last twenty years of his
life, he used only the back four rooms of his home. The front rooms he
used for storing everything from lawn mowers to worn-out brooms.

Adler may have been frugal at home, but he was exceedingly gen-
erous to his community. In 1939 he bought a pumper truck for the
local fire department, and over the years he made sure the firemen
had everything from ambulances to steak dinners and televisions to
watch on night duty. He also supported area hospitals, museums,
and sports teams, and paid for the construction of Baker City's baseball field and the local rodeo grounds. And when he died, in 1993,
Adler's entire $22 million estate was set aside for scholarships and
community projects throughout Baker County.

Visitors to Baker City can see Adler's legacy in many places.
There's Leo Adler Field and a paved path along the Powder River
called the Leo Adler Memorial Parkway. His home is now open to
the public as a museum, and some of his belongings, including sil-
verware, dishes, and a baseball, are on display at the Baker Heritage
Museum downtown. And every year the town celebrates Leo Adler
Days with a parade, a hot dog feed, and fireworks in his honor.

The Adler House is located at 2305 Main Street in Baker City and is open Friday through Monday. For information about hours and tours, call (541) 523-9308. For more information about Leo Adler and Adler-related landmarks, visit www.leoadler.com, call the Baker County Chamber of Commerce at (800) 523-1235, or go to www.visitbaker .com.

Eureka!
Baker City

Once you've visited the 80.4-ounce Armstrong Gold Nugget on display at the U.S. Bank branch here, you might be thinking about a new career as a gold prospector. Before you trade in your briefcase for a metal detector, donkey, and gold-panning equipment, though, you might want to pay a visit to the annual Miner's Jubilee, held each July in Baker City.

The festival celebrates the area's mining heritage and history with a parade, a rodeo, mining demonstrations, metal-detecting contests for kids and adults, and a street showing of *Paint Your Wagon*, the gold rush and gold miner–themed movie that was filmed in Baker County in 1968.

In the past the jubilee has featured everything from hand-mucking and rock-drilling contests to porcupine races and beard-growing competitions. These days, though, the crowds gather for ax-throwing contests, bingo games with gold nugget prizes, and the fast-paced Oregon State Gold Panning Competition, where the goal is to be the first to find three gold nuggets hidden in a gold pan full of diggings. No dawdling allowed: Both amateur and professional miners usually complete their "nugget recovery" in forty to fifty seconds; kids often complete the task in less than four minutes.

The Miner's Jubilee is held annually during the third weekend in July. Most events take place in Geiser Pollman Park in downtown Baker City. For details contact the Baker County Chamber of Commerce, at (800) 523-1235 or visit www.visitbaker.com.

Stringing Us Along
Burns

In among the cowboy photos, Native American artifacts, antique tools and other community treasures at the Harney County Historical Museum in Burns are a few curious gems.

In addition to sagebrush sandals that are more than 9,000 years old, there's a quilt with an ocean wave pattern, circa 1854, that was made

Some people hang onto sanity by a string.
Harney County Historical Museum

Meals for Miners

Mining history is full of tales of loners roaming the hills in search of the "Mother Lode." Some did strike it rich, although most prospectors were lucky if they made just enough to get by. Still, everyone had to eat. Essentials such as flour, salt, sugar, beans, potatoes, and coffee might make their way to remote mining camps on the back of a mule, but pretty much everything else had to come from the land. So in addition to panning for gold, miners hunted for wild game, caught fresh fish, and foraged for berries, fruit, and wild greens. Mining camps may not have offered many culinary conveniences, but if these recipes from the *Miner's Cookbook* are any indication, miners rarely starved, and some clearly seasoned their meals with plenty of humor.

Elephant Stew
Ingredients
1 elephant
2 rabbits (optional)
½ pail pepper
2 pails salt
4 bushels onions
93½ gallons water
6 pails flour

Cut elephant into bite-sized pieces. This should take about 4 months. Cook over kerosene fire for approximately 4 weeks or until tender. Add onions, cook until tender.

This will feed about 3,000 hungry miners. If more are expected, add the 2 rabbits. But do this only if necessary, as most people don't like hare in their stew.

Cougar Roast

(adapted by Lorrie Crawford, Merlin, Oregon)

Ingredients

4 to 5 pounds cougar shoulder roast

2 cloves garlic, sliced

bacon strips

garlic powder to taste

white vinegar

2 apples, cored and unpeeled

3 medium onions, sliced

4 tablespoons brown sugar

salt and pepper to taste

vegetable oil

butcher's string

When skinning the cougar try to make sure to keep as much hair as possible off the meat, as it is very fine and difficult to get off later. Debone roast and trim off all fat. Soak overnight in cold water which has salt and vinegar added to it. Next day, remove meat from soaking solution, dry well. Roll and tie with butcher's string. Coat roast with oil, then cook over high heat in a skillet or Dutch Oven to brown on all sides. Season with salt, pepper, garlic powder, and brown sugar. Place roast in the center of a large sheet. Put garlic cloves, onions, and apples around roast. Brush roast with oil and cover with bacon strips. Cook until tender.

Recipes from the *Miner's Cookbook* courtesy of the Eastern Oregon Mining Association

in Ohio. The pioneer family that brought the quilt out west claimed that some of the stitching was done by a young Abraham Lincoln.

The real curiosity here though, is this 265-pound, 40-inches-in diameter ball of string that sits covered with cellophane to keep it clean. Museum curators say the story in town is that after Mrs. Henry Seward lost a son in WWII, she took up saving string, instead of knitting, to maintain her sanity. She wound the string into this ball between February 1947 and December 1964.

The Harney County Historical Museum is at 18 West D Street in downtown Burns. For information and hours, call (541) 573-5618.

Fowl at Play
Burns

In the late 1800s, when feathered hats were the height of fashion, hunters had unrestricted access to the plumage of thousands of birds that used the lakes and marshes of southeastern Oregon as stopovers during migration.

That slaughter stopped in 1908 when President Theodore Roosevelt made the area a bird sanctuary. Now, each spring and fall, the 187,000-acre Malheur Refuge is a safe haven for hundreds of bird-watchers and as many as 100,000 nesting ducks, more than 5,000 white pelicans, and thousands of other birds, including Canada and snow geese, sandhill cranes, egrets, blue herons, great horned owls, golden eagles, and trumpeter swans, which have an impressive 7-foot wingspan.

There are spots along the Oregon coast where even more birds gather, but the variety of birds at the Malheur Refuge is impossible to beat. Officials say that more than 250 species can be regularly spotted here and, over the past century, 300-plus species have been sighted.

The Malheur National Wildlife Refuge is shaped like a T and is 40 miles long and 39 miles wide. A refuge headquarters with a visitor center and a museum with more than 250 bird specimens is located

Staring is allowed at the Grant County Museum.
Jayne L. Primrose

★ ★

on the south shore of Malheur Lake, about 32 miles southeast of
Burns. From Burns go south on OR 205 and then head east toward
New Princeton. For seasonal hours and additional information, call
(541) 493-2612 or go to www.fws.gov/malheur.

A good time to visit this area is during the John Scharff Migratory
Bird Festival, held each April in Burns. The festival includes guided
tours, an art show, lectures, and workshops on everything from making bird houses to taking bird pictures. For more information call
(541) 493-2612 or visit www.migratorybirdfestival.com.

Two Heads Are Better Than One
Canyon City

"Some people are appalled to hear we have two-headed calves and
the skulls of the first two people hanged in Canyon City," says Jayne
Primrose, the curator and manager of the Grant County Museum in
Canyon City. "But I just tell 'em Grant County is ranch country, and
we're just not politically correct out here." Then she laughs and adds,
"But the appalled folks are the ones who make a special trip just to
see them!"

Wouldn't you?

There are actually three sets of two-headed calves here: Two sets
are mounted like trophies on the wall, while the third set is a complete, awfully-cute taxidermied pair. "Kids just love 'em," says Primrose, "but the skulls—and their stories—are a bit more unnerving."

First, explains Primrose, you need to remember that gold was discovered in Canyon Creek in 1862 and, at the peak of the gold rush
sparked by that discovery, more than 10,000 people lived in Canyon
City, making it larger than Portland for quite some time. "Things
were rough in the early days, and hangings were legal," she says. But
not pleasant: On days when a hanging was scheduled, "the women
would gather up the children and leave town."

The skulls displayed at the museum are said to belong to Berry Way and William Cain. Both men were accused of murder, and it's unclear whether or not either of them got a fair trial before being hanged. Legend has it that Cain was almost nonchalant on his way to the gallows. According to a flyer at the museum, the doomed man "calmly played solitaire along the route" to the gallows, "handling the cards well despite his handcuffs." And when some young boys

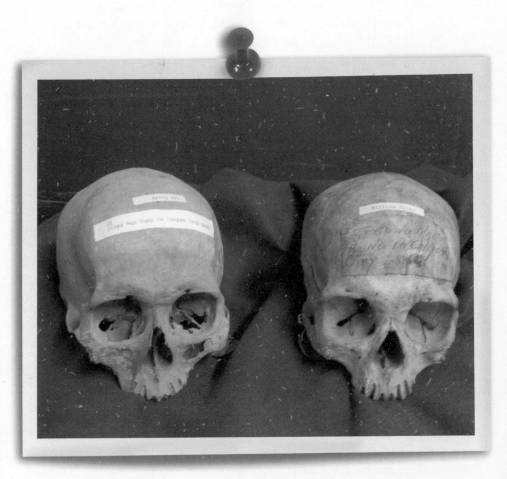

Crime didn't pay in early Canyon City.
Jayne L. Primrose

ran alongside the wagon, he reportedly told them, "Don't be in a hurry—there won't be anything doing until I get up there."

If you get to the museum, don't be in a hurry to leave once you've ogled the skulls and the two-headed calves. Less gruesome exhibits include gold nuggets, fossils and gemstones, and photographs of Charles W. Brown's Standard Oil Service Station, circa 1935. The town "junk" that Brown had on his office walls, including those skulls, now forms the core of the museum collection.

The Grant County Museum is open May through September and is located at 101 South Canyon City Boulevard (US 395) in Canyon City, about 2 miles south of John Day. For more information call (541) 575-0362 or visit http://ortclco.net/~museum.

Pomp's Circumstance
Danner

Jean Baptiste Charbonneau—nicknamed "Pomp" by Captain William Clark—was one of the most famous babies of the nineteenth century. Born in February 1805, Pomp was just two months old when his parents, Sacagawea and French-Canadian fur trader Toussaint Charbonneau, joined the Lewis and Clark Expedition.

Traveling on his mother's back, Pomp served as the expedition's cutest ambassador of peace, helping smooth relations between the Corps of Discovery and the Native American tribes they encountered along the way.

The well-traveled child grew up to be an ever-rambling adult. After the expedition the young Charbonneau lived in St. Louis for a while with William Clark, who later sent his young friend to boarding school. And when he turned eighteen, Charbonneau headed over to Europe as the guest of royalty, spending six years traveling and learning to speak at least four languages fluently.

When he returned to the States, Charbonneau found work as a mountain guide and scout, and at the end of his life was one of the many "49ers" trying to strike it rich in gold country. In fact, when he

★ ★

died, in 1866 at age sixty-one, he was at a stagecoach stop in south-eastern Oregon, on his way to the Montana gold fields. His traveling companions, no doubt dreaming of the gold they were missing, hastily sent off an obituary and left their buddy's body behind.

For years Charbonneau's grave site in remote Danner was unadorned, overgrown, unidentified, and ultimately forgotten. By the 1960s all the local ranchers knew was that there was a rumor about "someone famous" who was buried nearby. A determined historian eventually figured out whose grave that was, and in the early 1970s the grave site was cleaned up and placed on the National Register of Historic Places.

Today visitors will find a plaque and a protective fence by the grave site of the youngest member of the Lewis and Clark Expedition. The site is 3 miles north of US 95 on Danner Loop Road in Danner, 17 miles southwest of Jordan Valley.

Blast from the Past

Diamond

A dozen or so miles from Diamond there's a wild-horse viewing area where, if you're very lucky, you'll get to see one of the purest herds of Spanish mustangs existing in the world today. Unlike other wild horses, which are of mixed breeding, these Kiger mustangs still have the original characteristics of the Spanish Barb horses that were brought to North America by Spaniards in the sixteenth century.

Noted for their intelligence and stamina, and much sought after for adoption, the dun-colored Kiger mustangs have zebra-like stripes on their knees, hooked ear tips, bicolored manes and tails, and other distinctive markings. These mustangs were unknown until 1977, when a wild-horse specialist spotted some of them during a routine Bureau of Land Management wild-horse roundup. DNA tests showed these horses to be the real deal, and today two carefully monitored and managed herds of Kiger mustangs roam two separate BLM Herd Management Areas.

★ ★

Rare mustangs pose before heading back out on the range.
Bureau of Land Management/Oregon

To catch a glimpse of these beautiful rare horses out on the range, head east from Diamond for 6 miles on Happy Valley Road and then follow a dirt road several miles to the Kiger Mustang Viewing Area. Note that the road is only passable in dry weather (usually May through October) and is recommended only for four-wheel-drive, high-clearance vehicles. For more information contact the Harney County Chamber of Commerce at (541) 573-2636.

Cursed Cattle King

Diamond

Pete French was a ruthless but incredibly successful eastern Oregon cattle baron who started out as a ranch hand, married his boss's daughter, and ended up with one of the largest spreads in the

★ ★

West. At its peak, in the late 1800s, French's ranch spread out over 100,000 acres in Oregon's Lake and Harney Counties.

As he built his empire, though, French also built resentment among area businessmen and neighboring landowners who were evicted, often fraudulently, in his path. Years of disputes took a deadly turn on December 26, 1897, when French's neighbor, Ed Oliver, shot and killed him. He was arrested but quickly acquitted of the crime. Legend has it that Oliver wasn't just an angry neighbor, but also the unlucky chap who'd drawn the short straw in a local murder-for-hire plan.

Looking back, Pete French was not only a, shall we say, "creative" businessman, he was also an inventive architect. Around 1880 he built an unusual round barn that's 100 feet in diameter. Inside he

This unusual round barn once belonged to a really rough character. Bob Gibson, Blue Water Photography

Dave Crow's Wild Ride

You can visit the Pete French Round Barn alone, but if you're going to make the long trek out there, you might as well stop and visit with Dick Jenkins as well.

The Jenkins family settled here in 1880, and Dick Jenkins's grandfather bought the Round Barn from French's estate in 1916. Long used to store grain, the historic barn is now maintained by the state. But it's gregarious Dick Jenkins who keeps an eye on the place and who best knows the stories and secrets of the barn and most every structure and plot of land around here. His daylong historic, geological, wildlife, and heritage tours of the area often include a visit to the barn, but if you stop at the Round Barn Visitor Center and Museum when he's around, he'll happily regale you with stories like the one about Dave Crow's wild ride to Winnemucca, Nevada, after French's murder.

As Jenkins tells it, "Crow was a buckaroo on the ranch. He was there when French got killed and ended up being the one who had to go out and tell folks about it. The closest place with a Western Union teletype office was in Winnemucca, about 200 miles away. So Crow took off and got there in two days. He had to keep changing horses along the way, and while he didn't know what type of horse he'd get, he made sure to take his own bridle. And we have that bridle right here at our museum."

placed a 60-foot circular lava-rock corral so his cowboys could stay busy breaking and exercising horses during the severe southeastern Oregon winters. The impressive space has twelve tall juniper poles supporting the roof, which is covered with 50,000 shingles.

You can visit the Round Barn for free anytime during daylight hours at its remote spot about 20 miles northeast of Diamond, in what is now the southern section of the Malheur National Wildlife Refuge. From Diamond travel northeast on Happy Valley Road to the Round Barn Visitor

★ ★

Center, or drive northwest from Diamond on North Diamond Lane and then north on Lava Beds Road. You'll pass the Diamond Craters Recreation Area, which is a surreal-looking spot geologists say offers a rare chance to see diverse basaltic volcanic features in a relatively small space. The Round Barn is a half mile beyond the Round Barn Visitor Center and Museum. For more information call (888) 493-2420 or visit www.roundbarn.net.

Tons of Tractors
Enterprise

Whether or not you know the difference between a 1917 10-20 Titan or a 1925 Spoker D John Deere tractor, you'll definitely be surprised, overwhelmed, and charmed by the collection of vintage farm equipment and agricultural implements that grain farmer Erl McLaughlin has stuffed into the large metal building at Sunrise Iron, his Enterprise farm.

It's a hobby McLaughlin admits has turned into an obsession. "I've got thirty antique steel-wheel tractors, some horse-drawn vehicles, farm implements, more than seventy cast iron tractor seats, pictures, memorabilia and just lots of stuff," explains McLaughlin. "Most of it is here, but I've also got another building with more stuff about 10 miles from here."

McLaughlin doesn't just collect old rusty farm equipment; once he's located an item and rescued it, he restores it. "Between November and April, when I'm not farming, I've got a lot of time on my hands. So I spend that time working on the equipment. It's hard, grueling work sometimes to get things fixed and straightened out, but come spring I know I'll have something to show."

He knows he'll also have a few things that impress his wife. McLaughlin says sometimes when he hauls home yet another rusty antique tractor, his wife's first comment is that "it looks like the heels of bad luck." But when he cleans it up "she's the first to admit that it looks pretty darn nice."

This stuff cleans up awfully nice.
Vicky Searles

A great time to see Erl McLaughlin's collection of antique tractors and other agricultural implements is on the first weekend in August. That's when McLaughlin holds an open house and tractor show and invites fans of restored farm machinery to come by and demonstrate old engines and talk to visitors about how the equipment worked back in its time. Visitors are also welcome to stop by the farm, Sunrise Iron, any time of the year, as long as they call ahead to make an appointment. Sunrise Iron is located at 65708 Sunrise Road in Enterprise. For directions and information call (541) 426-4407 or see www.sunriseiron.com.

Mule Days
Enterprise

Billing itself as the "fastest growing mule show in the northwest" (so as not to be confused with those slow and stubborn ones?), the annual Hells Canyon Mule Days festival celebrates mules, donkeys, and the folks who just love hanging around these long-eared equines.

Why all this merrymaking for mules? "Because," says event organizer Sondra Lozier, "sure-footed asses were the major means of

The Fast Ass Express is one of the most popular events during Mule Days in Enterprise.
Tim Peters

★ ★

transportation for packers and outfitters during the settlement of the inhospitable terrain of the Hells Canyon area." Tough, sure-footed, "and very misunderstood," she says, "mules are finally getting some much-deserved recognition."

Well, at this event, they're at least the center of attention. In rodeo-style competitions, contestants show off their "mulemanship" in team roping, pole bending, barrel racing, and the Fast Ass Express, a relay race that's "always a favorite," says Lozier. Other events include wild cow milking, a flapjack race, and, for donkey-deprived kids, Stick Mule Races. To round out the fun, there's a non-motorized, mule-and-donkey-packed parade, cowboy poetry sessions, and prizes for both the oldest spectator and for the spectator who traveled the most miles to attend the show. Finally, there's a mule and horse sale at the end of the day.

Hells Canyon Mule Days is always held the weekend after Labor Day at the Wallowa County Fairgrounds, 101 South River Street, in Enterprise. For more information call (888) 323-3271 or go to www .hellscanyonmuledays.com. Enterprise is located in northeast Oregon, about 80 miles east of La Grande, on OR 82.

Dig That High School
Fossil

Lots of kids come home from school complaining that their teachers are "ancient." But students at Wheeler High School in Fossil have learned that "old," "ancient," and "over the hill" are very relative terms. That's because out behind the school's football field are the sedimentary remnants of a truly old lake that is now one of the world's rare public fossil beds. And it's chock-full of delicately preserved ferns, leaves, seeds, pods, and other extinct plants that are really ancient: more than thirty-three million years old.

While not fancy or highly publicized, these public fossil beds from the Oligocene period are particularly enticing. That's because just about 20 miles from Fossil is one section, or "unit," of the 14,000-acre John Day Fossil Beds National Monument, which is considered to contain the richest concentration of prehistoric mammalian and plant fossils in the world. More than 120 different species have been identified in the John Day Beds, and there's a fossil museum at the monument's Sheep Rock unit, but taking home even a tiny pebble from anywhere within the monument's grounds is strictly prohibited. So getting a chance to actually dig for your own fossils in the nearby town of Fossil is a rare treat.

The fossil beds in Fossil are extremely specimen-rich, so it's more than likely that anyone playing paleontologist-for-a-day in the crumbled shale will find something worth keeping. Most people find fossils of leaves and branches of ancestors of modern sycamore, maple, oak, alder, and other deciduous trees that grew along the adjacent stream banks, but once in a while something more unusual shows up.

Not sure how to dig or how to identify what you found? There's often a helpful and knowledgeable docent on duty. In addition, flyers are available that describe the most common fossils found here and offer tips on how to tap on the edges of the rocks just right so that they'll split cleanly apart to reveal the "surprise" fossil inside.

The public fossil beds at Wheeler High School in Fossil are located about 20 miles east of the Clarno area of the John Day Fossil Beds National Monument. Head east on OR 218 (Shaniko-Fossil Highway), then turn right onto OR 19 and right again onto Main Street. At Wheeler High School, drive around the school to the football field. The fossil beds are on an exposed bank directly beyond the football field and are open May through October. For more information about the public fossil beds and fossil-related activities in town, call Wheeler High School at (541) 763-4146 or the Oregon Paleolands Institute at (541) 763-4480; www.opli.org. For information about the John Day Fossil Beds, visit www.nps.gov/joda/index.htm.

Terminator Pigs and Mud Minnows

Most people digging in the public Wheeler High School fossil beds will find fossils of plants, but sometimes the fossils of ancient animals show up. These include mud minnows, salamanders, and frogs that lived in the ancient lake and a variety of animals that may have grazed, browsed, or quenched their thirst here. According to scientists from the Oregon Paleolands Institute, animal visitors probably included a catlike predator known as the "*pogonodon,*" a saber-toothed feline known as the "John Day tiger," and scary-sounding "terminator pigs," or *entelodonts,* which were wild boars that stood 6 feet high at the shoulders and had a "generally bad attitude."

The *Metasequoia,* or dawn redwood, a deciduous conifer, flourished in Oregon thirty-three to five million years ago and left its delicate mark embedded in rocks scattered about the Oregon landscape. Now the most common fossil found in the public fossil beds in the town of Fossil, the *Metasequoia* is a classic that had to wait until 2005 to be granted state fossil status.

Oregon's *Metasequoia* became extinct long ago, but paleontologists on a trip in a remote part of China more than fifty years ago were happy to encounter a live 100-foot *Metasequoia.* They brought specimens back to Oregon for propagation, ensuring that Oregon will have both live and fossilized versions of the tree for years—make that millions of years.

All the Way
Halfway

The town of Halfway (population about 335) is not, as its name may imply, in the center of Oregon. It's actually way over in the eastern part of the state, about 55 miles east of Baker City on OR 86 and halfway between the towns of Pine and Cornucopia. Still, when it comes to taking risks, the folks in Halfway are whole-hearted.

Tiny Halfway got national attention in the late 1990s during the Internet dot-com boom. Seeking a way to stand out from all the other start-up Internet companies, a Web-based company called Half.com was considering buying a few seconds of advertising time during the Super Bowl.

Halfway has a place in dot.com history.
Sue Forrester

Then someone came up with a better idea and contacted the mayor of the town of Halfway with an unusual, headline-grabbing offer: If the town agreed to change its name from Halfway to Half .com for one year, it would receive cash, computers for the schools, and a variety of other compensations, including design services for anyone in town who wanted their own Web site.

A deal was made, and the town of Halfway became Half.com. State road maps were altered to reflect the change, and Welcome to Half.com signs went up at the entrances to town. But six months later Half.com (the company) was sold to eBay, and eBay wasn't interested in renewing the contract.

That was back in 2001 (ancient times in the dot-com world), and while the school computers are now obsolete and the cash is long gone, former Halfway mayor, Gordon Kaesemeyer, still thinks his predecessor made a good decision. "We used some of the money to buy the town a snow plow, and we still have that. And some of the money was used to seed a community development corporation, and that has netted lots of ideas and more than a million dollars worth of projects for our little town. So you can't say it was a silly thing for us to do."

And there were those two entrance signs welcoming people to Half.com. One of them went to the Pine Valley Community Museum. The *Hells Canyon Journal* reported that in 2007 the town sold the other sign on eBay for a thousand dollars.

Golden Flower of Prosperity
John Day

It's a little hard to imagine when looking at it now, but the tiny old building that housed Kam Wah Chung & Co. (the name translates loosely as "Golden Flower of Prosperity") was once the social and religious center of the Chinese community in eastern Oregon. It also served as a trading post for cowboys, miners, and pioneers; an herbal medical office; a Chinese temple; a bunkhouse; and an opium den.

This building once housed a general store and an opium den.
Oregon Parks and Recreation Department

From 1888 until 1948 the building's lease was held by Doc Hay and Lung On, two of thousands of Chinese immigrants who came to the John Day and Canyon City area after gold was discovered here. Lung On operated a general store selling everything from mining supplies and dry goods to the region's first automobiles. He also had bootleg whiskey available during Prohibition. Doc Hay was a master herbalist, well known for his skills of pulse diagnosis and successful treatments. His apothecary of more than 500 herbs ranged from common clove, ginger, and wild asparagus to bear claws, chicken gizzards, and dried lizards.

The business partners lived and worked here and, at times, so did relatives, friends, and itinerants. The seven-room building held

★ ★

two bedrooms, a bunkroom, and, in the back, two rooms set up for smoking opium.

No one knows exactly why, but one day in 1948 the businesses and the building, with all the contents intact, were simply closed and shuttered. Nothing was touched for twenty years, until 1968 when a group of volunteers went in, carefully removed and cleaned every single item, and replaced everything exactly as it was found.

Today the unusual and somewhat mysterious building is both a memorial and a museum. The apothecary and general store is filled with tin containers, wooden boxes, foodstuffs, tobacco, and medicinal products, including jars and jars (and jars) of herbs, some desiccated fruit that's been sitting there since 1949, and a snake in a bottle. Adhered to the walls are pieces of paper lettered in Chinese script. Two of the translated messages read, "Wealth comes and even expands," and, "Friends fill the doors—friends like clouds."

Doc Hay and Lung On were known for extending hospitality, especially to other Chinese immigrants making the transition to life in America. But clearly not everyone who bunked here was a friend. In the bedroom, alongside Chinese antiques and other furnishings, is the cleaver Doc Hay kept on his bed stand.

The museum and an adjacent visitor center are open daily May through October, just off US 26 in John Day. For more information call (541) 575-2800 or (800) 551-6949 or visit www.oregonstate parks.org/park_8.php.

Watch Out for Wally

Joseph

The folks in Scotland may have "Nessie," the Loch Ness Monster, and people in Canada may be enamored with Ogopogo, the monster said to live in British Columbia's Lake Okanagan. But why break out the passport when there's a perfectly good seldom-seen creature in a lovely lake right here in eastern Oregon?

Affectionately dubbed "Wally," this horned, multilegged, bovine water beast supposedly makes his home in Wallowa Lake, which at 5,000 feet in elevation is the highest body of water in eastern Oregon. Legends about this monster date back to the Nez Perce Indians who lived along the shores of the lake, and the creature has been variously described as being anywhere from 10 feet to more than 100 feet long and looking like a Chinese dragon with the head of a hog or a giant sharklike fish with a rounded nose.

The story of the Wallowa Lake Monster really "grew legs," as they say, in November 1885, when a white settler claiming to have encountered the creature told his story to the local paper, the *Wallowa County Chieftain*. According to the original newspaper report, a prospector "who refuses to give his name to the public" had been out on the lake shortly after dusk when he encountered a strange creature that "reared its head and neck up out of the water ten or twelve feet," made a "low bellow something like that of a cow," and appeared to be "one hundred feet in length." Although the light was low and "it was too dark to see the animal distinctly," the prospector admitted, "it seemed to have a large, flat head. Something like that of a hippopotamus, and its neck, which was about ten feet in length, was as large around as a man's body."

Though not nearly as detailed, occasional "Wally" sightings have been reported throughout the years. And while modern-day scientists flock to the lake because of its unusual geologic formation, many other "researchers" head here hoping for an encounter with the Wallowa Lake Monster.

Wallowa Lake is part of Wallowa Lake State Park and is located in the northeastern corner of Oregon, just off OR 82, 6 miles south of Joseph. For more information call the Wallowa County Chamber of Commerce at (800) 585-4121 or go to www.oregonstateparks.org/park_27.php.

★ ★

Swiss-Style Ride

Joseph

If you have no luck finding Wally, the Wallowa Lake Monster, lake-side, try a view from above—way above—looking down from a gon-dola on the Wallowa Lake Tramway.

When it was built in 1970, the tramway was the steepest vertical gondola ride in North America. "It may still be," say tramway opera-tors, but when the season is in full swing, they're too busy to keep track of the competition.

Steepest or not, the tramway is a Swiss-made engineering marvel, with a 150-horsepower electric motor at the base powering a single continuous-loop cable that's almost 4 miles long. Four-passenger gondolas climb nearly 4,000 feet in fifteen minutes, from the 4,450-foot base of Mount Howard to its 8,150-foot summit. At the top,

Tram Facts

- **Highest point off ground: 120 feet (between towers four and five)**
- **Lowest point off ground: 3 feet (between towers seventeen and eighteen)**
- **Highest tower: tower four at 74 feet**
- **Cable length: 19,300 feet (nearly 4 miles long)**
- **When constructed, this tram was the steepest vertical lift in North America.**
- **There are twenty-five towers total and a 3,700-foot rise from base to summit.**

Tramway facts courtesy Wallowa Lake Tramway.

Bring binoculars for a chance to see the lake monster.
Wallowa County Chamber of Commerce

and along the way, riders are rewarded with spectacular views of the Wallowa Valley and the Wallowa mountain range ("The Wallowas"), known as the "Alps of Oregon."

At the summit there's a snack bar, gift shop, and several hiking paths leading to view points where it is possible to see into parts of Washington, Idaho, and, on a very clear day, sections of Montana. Eagle-eyed and very imaginative folks may also be able to make out the shadows of a 100-foot-long monster in Wallowa Lake as well.

The Wallowa Lake Tramway is located at the south end of Wallowa Lake at 59919 Wallowa Lake Highway in Joseph. It's open May through September and offers a limited winter schedule. For more information call (541) 432-5331 or visit www.wallowalaketramway.com.

★ ★

Lost Soles
Juntura

Head east from the tiny town of Juntura on US 20 toward the tinier town of Harper, and keep your eyes open between mileposts 206 and 207 for this most unusual tree. It's some sort of willow tree, but unlike any willow we've seen elsewhere, this one blooms year-round with shoes.

Peer into the branches and you're likely to see old sneakers and shabby slippers, tiny baby shoes, worn-out hiking boots, and the occasional ski boot. Kathy Bertalotto and her husband drive by this tree a lot and have watched it transform from a "regular" tree into a footwear-full tree. "It started with just two pairs of shoes, a pair of women's dress shoes and a pair of men's tennis shoes. Then it

Is that a good pair of size-5 running shoes up there?
Kiefer Davis

really began to sprout shoes, and it's now laced with shoes" of every type. "One branch even broke from the weight of the shoes," says Bertalotto.

No one knows for sure why people began filling this tree with shoes. Some say students from an area high school started it to ward off boredom. But Bertalotto prefers to believe this legend: "A weary traveler with worn shoes walking on a highway stopped at a tree by the roadside. He looked up and saw a pair of shoes just his size hanging in a tree and put them on. Grateful for the new shoes and for the subsequent improvements in his life, the traveler started a shoe tree in another area to help another lost soul."

Whether you believe that story or just find a tree full of shoes an entertaining sight, make sure you check around for rattlesnakes when you get out of the car to take a picture or to make a contribution to the tree.

But this isn't the only shoe tree in eastern Oregon. Out on the highway between Mitchell and John Day, there's another one. It's on US 26 at about Milepost 88. And all folks know (or will say) about this shoe tree is that about fifteen years ago someone spotted one pair of shoes up in that tree. Now the tree is covered in footwear; everything from dress shoes, sneakers, and loafers, to bowling shoes, ski boots and cowboy boots.

Big Attraction; Small Town
Mitchell

The biggest attraction in the four-block town of Mitchell is Henry. In fact, at 700 pounds Henry may just be the biggest thing in this tiny town.

Hugh Reid, a big bear of a guy himself, adopted Henry from a bankrupt private zoo when the bear was just one year old. Ever since then, Henry the bear and Hugh the person have been best friends.

The bear lives in a big enclosure right next to the town's service station, which is owned by Hugh Reid, who's usually nearby, in a

★ ★

crisp white t-shirt. "The bear is as gentle as a puppy," says former mayor Kiefer Davis, "You can kiss him and hug him and take pictures with him. And Hugh even lets people go in there and feed the bear an apple or something. I don't think Henry even realizes he is a bear."

Sometimes it's a bear being man's best friend.
Kiefer Davis

A Fungus among Us

In 1999 scientists in eastern Oregon were trying to figure out what was killing tree after tree in one section of the Malheur National Forest. What they discovered landed them in the *Guinness Book of World Records*—and proves that truth is stranger than fiction. Or at least stranger than some of the things you see in science-fiction movies.

The tree killer turned out to be a mushroom. Not just any mushroom, but the World's Largest Mushroom. Officially known as *Armillaria ostoyae*, or honey mushroom, this formidable fungus stretches out 3.5 miles, across an area equivalent to 1,600 football fields. Its tentacles, called rhizomorphs, have been spreading underground for anywhere from 2,500 to 8,000 years, sucking water and nutrients from tree roots and leaving behind thirsty timbers. Tiny bits of the mushroom peek out here and there in the forest, like tantalizing tips of icebergs, but the behemoth body of the fungus hides 3 feet underground. After careful study and long debate, scientists and the *Guinness Book of World Records* have dubbed this the largest living organism on earth.

Monster mushrooms aren't all that rare. Before scientists found this humongous fungus, the world's largest organism was another *Armillaria ostoyae*. But that one covers just 1,500 acres near Mt. Adams in Washington State.

All Hopped Up
Milton-Freewater

Not everyone was happy when the tiny eastern Oregon towns of Milton and Freewater merged back in the 1950s. For years there'd been good-natured competition between the citizens of the two towns, but most everyone was appalled when vandals changed the wording on the new sign at the edge of town from WELCOME TO MILTON-FREEWATER to WELCOME TO MUDDY FROGWATER.

★ ★

A good place to get toad in Milton-Freewater.
City of Milton-Freewater

People were upset, but then town officials decided Muddy Frog-water had a ring, or maybe a ribbit, to it. And so for more than twenty-five years now there's been a Muddy Frogwater Festival in Milton-Freewater. The three-day event includes a parade, a Pretty

★ ★

Baby Contest (judges are recruited from out of town, "for their own protection"), and the ever-popular frog-jumping contest.

In the early days of the festival, people would bring their own home-groomed jumpers to the races in jars, boxes, and sacks. "But it's very hot around here," says Cheryl York of the Milton-Freewater Chamber of Commerce, "and sometimes the frogs didn't make it. So now we fly in special jumping frogs and frog handlers from Texas. It works out much better." And York says once the frogs finish racing, they get to retire in a stream nearby where "they live happily ever after."

The frog frenzy in Milton-Freewater doesn't fall off after the frog festival. Not long ago the city decided to "go green" and promote itself as a "Toadly Awesome Place to Live." The amphibian-loving town has laced its downtown with almost fifty frog sculptures and frog-festooned murals. And many of the frogs fit right in: There's a frog in front of the library reading a book, a frog on crutches outside a chiropractor's office, a frog up on a light pole taking care of the lines, and frogs around town that can be spotted cooking, golfing, and skateboarding. Armed with frog-spotting maps, frog-fans from out of town can be found pulling over in their cars and jumping out to get their pictures taken with each frog.

To encourage the frog infestation, the city sponsors a "Logs to Frogs" chain saw–carving competition each July and has a formal program to help merchants purchase frog statues for their businesses. There's even a plan to open a frog museum with all the frog-related paraphernalia that's been hopping into City Hall. Feeling froggy? The Muddy Frogwater Country Classic Festival and Corn Roast is held each August at Richard Yantis Memorial Park. You can see the frog statues around town year-round with the help of a "frog locator" map available at City Hall and at the Milton-Freewater Chamber of Commerce at 505 Ward Street. To get there, follow the Information Center signs from OR 11. For more information call (541) 938-5563 or go to www.mfchamber.com.

★ ★

Jailhouse Jeans
Pendleton

Forget the license plates. At the medium-security Eastern Oregon
Correctional Institution in Pendleton, the 1,500 inmates can earn
money working in the laundry or in the woodshop, crafting toys,
clocks, and other items for local charities and civic groups. But since
1989 the jobs most coveted by the murderers, rapists, and other con-
victs doing time here center around sewing.

Don't snicker. Well, don't let any of the inmates hear you snicker.

These jobs are harder to get than a pardon or early parole. And
the fifty to sixty inmates lucky enough to snag a position at the

**Don't be blue about buying clothes "Made on the
Inside to be Worn on the Outside."**
Leslie Carnes, Pendelton Chamber of Commerce

on-site Prison Blues garment factory not only get paid a good wage, they learn how to operate professional sewing machines and work on every aspect of garment production, from pattern conception to quality inspection, inventory control, and shipping.

Like the inmates themselves, the Prison Blues clothing line is described as being tough as nails, and is worn by folks in jail—and out. Marketed worldwide under the slogan "Made on the Inside to be Worn on the Outside," the inmate-made jeans, yard coats, T-shirts, and work shirts have become popular items with everyone from cowboys and construction workers to fashion-conscious teenagers in Japan. The line even has a "celebrity" endorser, Oregon-born lumberjack champion Rob Waibel.

Since the Prison Blues garments are made in prison, it's not really possible to tour the factory or shop in a factory store. But the products are sold online and in many retail outlets, including the Correction Connection at 27 Southeast Court Avenue in downtown Pendleton. For more information call the shop at (541) 276-1169 or www.correctionconnectionprisonblues.com. You can also visit the Prison Blues Web site at www.prisonblues.com.

Underground Undercover

Pendleton

For years folks came to Pendleton seeking the authentic Wild West woven into blankets at the Pendleton Woolen Mill and whooped up by rodeo cowboys during the annual Pendleton Round Up.

Little was known about the Wild West memories locked up in the 70-plus miles of tunnels crisscrossing beneath Pendleton's historic district. Old-timers in town knew about these tunnels, but for a long time people were embarrassed about what had gone on there. In the late 1980s, however, some of these tunnels were opened up and restored and now serve as one of the town's main attractions.

The history of the tunnels is not a pretty story. According to historians, they were dug in the late 1870s as living quarters by and for

Chinese laborers seeking refuge from discrimination aboveground. In use until the 1930s, the tunnels eventually housed a wide variety of illegal activities, including card rooms and saloons where bartenders were paid in gold dust, an opium den, bordellos, and a Prohibition speakeasy with secret escape routes. At times legal "aboveground" businesses operated underground as well, including laundries and bathhouses, an ice plant, a butcher shop, and an ice-cream parlor that remained open until 1933.

Today there are regular tours of the underground that end up aboveground, at Miss Stella's impressively-preserved Cozy Room bordello. At one time Pendleton was home to eighteen bordellos, and

Active Underground

Twice a year the Pendleton Underground "Comes to Life." More than seventy-five actors dress up as old-time card players, dancers, bartenders, cowboys, Chinese workers, and merchants for a two-hour reenactment of what life might have been like in the underground and in the street-side bordellos in the days when Pendleton's 3,000 residents supported thirty-two saloons and eighteen houses of ill repute.

Guests are encouraged to interact with the actors (in a non–X-rated way, of course), and it's a hoot and a holler to see everyone stay in character. The event is a fund-raiser held each May and is so popular that tickets usually sell out shortly after they go on sale in February.

Call Portland Underground Tours at (800) 226-6398 for more information.

one of them now operates as the Working Girls Hotel. Restored and furnished in Victorian decor, the five-room hotel offers amenities such as air-conditioning, large bathrooms, and hardwood floors, but no "traditional" bordello services.

The Pendleton Underground Tours are offered year-round, with a restricted winter schedule. The tours start at Southwest First Street and Emigrant Avenue, in Pendleton's downtown historic district. The Working Girls Hotel is at 17 Southwest Emigrant, just a few doors down from the Pendleton Underground Tours offices. For more information, call (800) 226-6398 or visit www.pendletonunder groundtours.org.

Once a year the Pendleton Underground comes alive.
Leslie Carnes, Pendelton Chamber of Commerce

★ ★

Creature Comforts
Ukiah

In a small town like Ukiah (population 250) it's hard to miss the Antlers Inn. But even in a bigger town it would be hard to miss because nailed to the front of the hotel are racks and antlers from perhaps a hundred deer, elk, moose, and caribou. Inside, it's a veritable menagerie.

"The first thing me and my partners did when we bought the place," says Scott Atkinson, "was nail up all the antlers we could find. We had a lot of our own, but then friends and townspeople brought over more. The other thing we did was change the name. And 'inn' just sounds more prestigious to me than a hotel."

Prestigious? Built in the 1870s as a boardinghouse, the former Ukiah Prairie Hotel once served as a stage stop between Pendleton and John Day. Atkinson and his partners bought the place in the

Put a little wildlife in your life.
Scott Atkinson

No doubt about it—it's the Antlers Inn.
Scott Atkinson

1980s after they drove into town after a hunting trip and had to wait behind a dozen other hunters for a chance to wash up in the hotel's walk-in showers. "Once we owned it, we didn't have to wait in line."

Today the Antlers Inn, in the heart of elk and deer country, is still quite rustic, "although we did buy new beds," says Atkinson. There are two shared bathrooms and a dozen guest rooms, some of which still have their original wallpaper. The inn also offers amenities you won't find at any boutique urban hotels, including a walk-in cooler that holds up to ten elk and a gathering spot called the Bull Room, where guests chat and watch TV in the company of animal skulls, a taxidermied grizzly bear, the mounted head of a wolf, trophy elk racks, and the skins of various mountain creatures.

The Antlers Inn is located on Main Street in Ukiah, 55 miles south of La Grande on OR 244. For more information call (541) 427-3492.

★ ★

Cowboy on Duty
Umatilla

With his broad shoulders, red-striped shirt, blue boots, and necker-chief, this gun-toting, 35-foot tall John Wayne-ish looking cowboy has served as a landmark for the folks of Umatilla ever since 1954. "They use him to give directions," says Bill Meade, who got the cowboy with the grocery store he bought back in 1992. "They'll say 'go two blocks past the cowboy' and things like that. He's definitely part of this town. And if I ever considered taking him down or selling him I'd be run out of town."

The Umatilla cowboy (he looks the same on both sides) is located outside Columbia Harvest Foods at 1411 Sixth Street in downtown Umatilla. Swing by and say howdy.

Betcha' this cowboy has some of that steak on his shopping list.
Dave Meade–Harvest Foods

✦ ✦

Hog Feed and Rat Shoot

Unity

If life gives you an infestation of rodents, round 'em up and have a party.

At least that's what they do in and around the tiny town of Unity each year. And they have a hoot and a holler and a hog feed while they're at it.

According to Kathy Endicott, owner of Unity's Eldorado Ditch Bar Co. Restaurant and Lounge, the whole thing started with ground squirrels. "These aren't those cute, bushy-tailed animals. We consider them rats." Endicott says the ground squirrels wreak havoc on area ranches. "They carry diseases. They eat the alfalfa crops. And they make holes in the ground that cows and horses step in and break their legs. And the rats make tunnels underground that ruin everyone's gardens."

Over the years ranchers have tried poisoning the rodents, but that's expensive and can lead to other problems. So Endicott, who is affectionately known around here as the "Eastern Oregon Rat Queen," organizes an annual Hog Feed and Rat Shoot each year. "It's a community service and a way for us to have a good time."

Here's how it works: As many as thirty-five six-person teams each get assigned to shoot ground squirrels on a different ranch. The goal is simply to shoot as many ground squirrels as possible between 8 a.m. and 4 p.m. "It's not hard to do," says Endicott. "You can just sit in a lawn chair and shoot and do quite well."

At the end of the day, dead squirrels are gathered up in buckets and counted by volunteers from the high school. (Tipping is allowed, but it won't change the count.) The competition is good-natured but fierce. In 2006 the winning team bagged 620 ground squirrels, and more than 13,000 rodents were eliminated overall.

In addition to the satisfaction of helping out area ranchers, winning teams get prizes that range from locally crafted leather goods and juniper-wood trophies to a taxidermied ground squirrel. And at

★ ★

A pesky ground squirrel is sort of cute—when it's dead.
Heidi Lagao, Kolshots Photography; Kolshots.com

the end of the day, every hunter is invited to sit down to a roast pig dinner.

The dead squirrels end up as dinner for coyotes and wild birds.

The Unity Hog Feed and Rat Shoot is held each year during the last weekend in April. If you're planning to join in, get your name on the list early. Kathy Endicott says there's usually a long waiting list of teams hoping to participate. There's no waiting, however, to see the photos and memorabilia from past events on display year-round at the Eldorado Ditch Bar Co. Restaurant and Lounge at 401 Job Creek Road in Unity.

Unity is located between John Day and Baker City. Take OR 7 south of Baker City to OR 245. Head south and then west on 245, then east on US 26 to Unity. For more information call (541) 446-3447, and ask to speak with the Eastern Oregon Rat Queen.

index

index

index

index

index

index

index

★ ★

Harriet Baskas is the author of six travel books, including *Washington Curiosities* and *Washington Icons* for Globe Pequot Press. She's built and managed several community radio stations in Oregon and Washington and is an award-winning public radio producer. Her columns about airports and air travel appear on www.MSNBC.com, www.USAToday.com, and a variety of other outlets, including her blog, www.StuckattheAirport.com.